M000016810

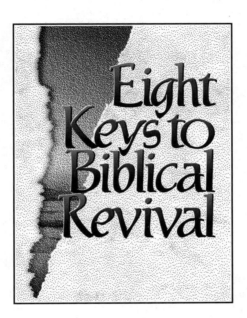

Eight Keys to Biblical Revival

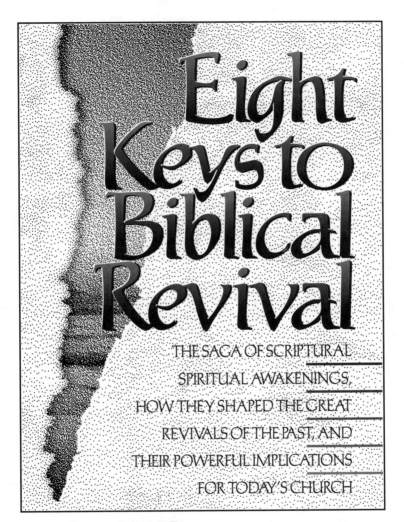

Eight Keys to Biblical Revival

THE SAGA OF SCRIPTURAL
SPIRITUAL AWAKENINGS,
HOW THEY SHAPED THE GREAT
REVIVALS OF THE PAST, AND
THEIR POWERFUL IMPLICATIONS
FOR TODAY'S CHURCH

LEWIS DRUMMOND

BETHANY HOUSE PUBLISHERS
Minneapolis, Minnesota 55438

DR. LEWIS DRUMMOND has fifteen books to his credit and a wide list of accomplishments. He has taught and lectured in seminaries and colleges across the nation and throughout the world. He has served as the President of Southeastern Baptist Theological Seminary and is presently the Billy Graham Professor of Evangelism and Church Growth at Beeson Divinity School.

"If my people, who are called by my name, will humble themselves and pray and seek my face and turn from their wicked ways, then will I hear from heaven and will forgive their sin and will heal their land."

2 CHRONICLES 7:14

INTRODUCTION

The heart-cry for revival ascends from every quarter. Not for decades has there been such interest, even *burden*, for a refreshing spiritual awakening. Billy Graham recently asked a university professor what he thought was the greatest need of our hour. After careful consideration, the professor responded: "I could give you a variety of answers all the way from tax relief to disarmament. I may surprise you, because I'm not a religious man, but I believe that the greatest need that we have at this hour is a spiritual awakening which will restore individual and collective morals and integrity throughout the nation." The professor's perception is pervasive; everywhere God's people resonate with James: "Behold, the farmer waits for the precious produce of the soil, being patient about it, until it gets the early and late rains" (James 5:7, NASB). For that "latter rain" we plead. Thankfully, the heavens do seem heavy just waiting for God to reach down into His bottomless resource of blessings, draw out a jagged streak of awakening grace and pierce the pregnant clouds, sending a deluge of revival blessings on us.

Yet this heart-cry for revival is not new. History has heard it repeatedly. The Bible itself abounds with promises concerning revival. The Scriptures make it abundantly clear that spiritual awakening has been part and parcel of God's gracious dealings with His people through the ages. But a fundamental question arises: What constitutes a genuine spiritual awakening? The thrust of this book attempts to answer that basic query from God's Holy Word. The Scriptures form the final authoritative source for any and all spiritual reality. It alone, therefore, defines the essence of a true revival. And, moreover, the Word of God will inspire us to seek such a movement of the Spirit today.

The biblical inquiry shall not be undertaken from a technically critical perspective, although biblical clarity and careful exegesis is sought. It attempts to arrive at *practical* scriptural answers concerning the nature of revivalism and spiritual awakening. But there is a decided spin-off from searching the Word in this fashion: When we discover what the Scriptures state experientially and pragmatically concerning revival, we shall hopefully be moved to seek an awakening in our time. If that takes place, the effort put into writing this volume will be well worth it all.

Gratitude must be expressed to my faithful secretaries at Southeastern Baptist Theological Seminary in Wake Forest, North Carolina, and Beeson Divinity School at Samford University, Birmingham, Alabama. They spent much time and energy on the manuscript. Many friends, too numerous to mention, have helped me in my quest to understand and experience revival. For them I am thankful. May God bless us all and give us spiritual awakening in our day.

Lewis A. Drummond
Birmingham, Alabama
1994

CONTENTS

The Anatomy of a Spiritual Awakening

The times of refreshing from the presence of the Lord have at last dawned upon our land. Everywhere there are signs of aroused activity and increased earnestness. A spirit of prayer is visiting our churches, and its paths are dropping fatness. The first breath of the rushing wind is already discerned, while on rising evangelists the tongues of fire have evidently descended.[1]

With these intriguing words, Charles Haddon Spurgeon, the incomparable Victorian London preacher, described the refreshing spiritual awakening that engulfed his early ministry. What a time it must have been for the powerful pulpiteer! What was actually taking place?

The erupting spirit of revival, or spiritual awakening, as such movements are variously termed, had moved across the Atlantic to Great Britain from America where it was already ignited and spreading from coast to coast.* When it swept onto Britain's shores it initially sparked Ireland. In 1858 the Presbyterian Church of Ireland had dispatched observers to the United States to investigate what was already being called the "Prayer Revival." The spirit of renewal had virtually engulfed the entire American nation and was making news worldwide. The Irish observers returned home renewed, and began to thrill others with what they had experienced. Soon Belfast, Dublin, Cork, and the entire countryside fell under the impact of the prayer movement. Ireland sank to its knees in intercession. The spirit of the Old Testament "solemn assembly" sounded forth and the saints responded.

---

*The very first "wind of the Spirit" had an early, germinal beginning in Canada in 1857.

Wales also began to feel the breath of the Spirit—almost simultaneously with Ireland. Before long all of Wales caught fire with awakening power.

As the continuing news and challenging stories of the awakening spread throughout the British Isles, Scotland roused itself to the call of the Spirit. Prayer meetings sprang up in Glasgow and Edinburgh; soon all the cities and towns of the country responded. By 1859 the United Presbyterian Church reported that one fourth of its members regularly attended prayer meetings for spiritual awakening.

Finally, England took notice and began to be warmed by the conflagration. In 1859 a united prayer meeting was launched in the Throne Room of the Cosby Hall, London. Attendance soon reached one hundred at the noon-hour service. By the end of the year, twenty-four daily and sixty weekly prayer meetings dotted the London area. In a matter of days, the number escalated to one hundred twenty; then the revival fire spread throughout the entire English countryside.

As 1860 was ushered in, the Fortune, Garrick, and Sadler Wells theaters of London opened their doors for Sunday evangelistic services. Even the very traditional Saint Paul's and Westminster Cathedrals scheduled special revival services. The ministry of Charles H. Spurgeon spread into full bloom as the mammoth Metropolitan Tabernacle, Spurgeon's new church building, neared completion.

In Dorset, people flocked to hang on every word of Evan Hopkins. He later became a key figure in the significant Keswick Conventions. Charles G. Finney, the great American revivalist, preached with tremendous effect in Bolton as the revival deepened over England. William and Catherine Booth of Salvation Army fame ministered with fresh power. Oxford and Cambridge Universities commenced special meetings. Britain, it seemed, had prostrated itself before God in fervent prayer.

As could be expected, the awakening created its caustic critics. The secularists voiced their vindictives in chorus as they attempted to negate the positive impact of the movement. But historians now realize the awakening left a legacy of blessing extending even to this day. During the revival one million new members entered the ranks of the British churches. Not only that, the Salvation Army, the Children's Special Service Mission, the China Inland Mission, and a host of new institutions and benevolent movements were founded that still carry on. As Spurgeon put it:

> It were well . . . that the Divine life would break forth everywhere—in the parlor, the workshop, counting house, the market, and streets. We are far too ready to confine it to the channel of Sunday services and religious meetings; it deserves a broader floodway and we must have it if we are to see gladder times. It must burst out upon men who do not care for it, and invade chambers where it will be regarded as an intrusion; it must be seen by wayfaring men streaming down the places of traffic and concourse, *hindering the progress of sinful trades*, and surrounding all, whether they will or no. Would to God that religion were more vital and forceful among us, so as to create *a powerful public opinion* on behalf of truth, justice, and holiness. . . . A life that would *purify the age*. It is much to be desired that the Christian church may yet have *more power and influence* all over the world for *righteousness . . . social reform, and moral progress.*[2]

Such social and moral reforms are what a spiritual awakening can accomplish. And that is what Britain experienced in 1860. The refreshing revival season had arrived. The Prayer Revival will always stand as a classic illustration of a true awakening. But the question still surfaces: What actually takes place, in *principle* and in *final results*, during revival times? Perhaps even more important, what produces a great awakening? The answers, of course, rest in the Scriptures: Therefore, we must turn to the Word of God. There the accounts of several fascinating revivals are found, which exemplify the principles of revival.

As we begin our biblical odyssey, seeking to travel the routes of revival, James Burns in his classic work *Revivals, Their Laws and Leaders* points us in the right direction, instructing us to look for several principles that normally cluster around a spiritual awakening. Of course, the Bible itself must give us the full and final answer concerning the nature of an awakening. Yet, Burns' concepts can serve at least as a preliminary signpost in our search for what the Word of God reveals concerning a true revival.

A brief explanatory note is in keeping at this point concerning definitions and terminology. There are those who would draw a rather sharp, definitive line between revival and spiritual awakening. They hold that *revival* occurs among the people of God as they repent and spiritual vitality is restored. Then, they tell us, *spiritual awakening* sweeps the general community and many are converted. Of course, such a distinction can be properly made; however, most works on the phenomenon use the two terms interchangeably. The words have certainly been employed synonymously throughout the history of revival. Even the term *renewal* is at times used in the same manner. Therefore, it seems wise in this study to take the more historic, traditional stance and use the terms interchangeably. At the same time, it certainly is the case that God first awakens His own saints and restores and renews them before significant change occurs in the community. The principles Burns sets forth will make that clear.

Burns' Principles of Spiritual Awakenings*

The Principle of the Fullness of Time

A revival awakens the church to the reality that God controls His work and will give His people what they need when they need it. God is recognized as sovereign. He gives an awakening when His sovereign will pleases. A revival may come quite suddenly and virtually unexpected by the church at large, but God orders all the details. He is Lord of the harvest.

The Principle of the Emergence of the Prophet

Revivals usually produce great leaders. There have been exceptions, like the Prayer Revival of 1858–1860 that was largely led by laypeople. Still, normally one or more significant leaders emerge in the movement. A classic illustration is George Whitefield and John Wesley in the Eighteenth-Century Revival in Britain.

---

*Burns' principles are discussed in detail in the author's previous work on revival, *The Awakening That Must Come* (Broadman Press, 1978).

The Law of Progress in Spiritual Matters

A revival first and foremost generates new spiritual life as it surges through the church and community. Evangelism, social action, a new awareness of spirituality, etc., always surfaces. Spirituality superceding materialism becomes paramount.

The Principle of Variety

Every revival reveals a uniqueness of its own. No awakening manifests itself identically in detail with any other movement, even though the same basic principles invariably arise. For example, the Prayer Revival centered on prayer, while the Eighteenth-Century Awakening revolved around great preaching. The Welsh Revival of 1904–1906 featured singing and testimony.

The Principle of Recoil

Revivals come to an end. Sad, but true! Martin Luther said that thirty years constitutes the outer limit of an awakening. Whether he was invariably right or not, the sun finally sets in every revival.

The Principle of Theology

Theology changes during revival times, often rather radically. The church returns to basic, conservative evangelical thought, apostolic simplicity and doctrine.

The Principle of Consistency

Although revivals obviously differ; yet, certain vital spiritual elements always surface. This we shall discover as we examine various biblical awakenings.

Packer's Views

J. I. Packer, in his helpful book *Keep in Step With the Spirit*, points out the following elements in a true awakening:

1. Revival is God revitalizing His church.
2. Revival is God turning His anger away from His church.
3. Revival is God stirring the hearts of His people.
4. Revival is God displaying the sovereignty of His grace.[3]

In essence, the church becomes revitalized, the community is touched and changed, needs are met, lives experience change, longings are fulfilled, and great glory is ascribed to God. Can there be any doubt that we need such a movement in our times? Gerald R. McDermott put his finger right on the spot when he said,

> Evangelicals are frustrated because their attempts to transform American culture seem to have failed. After electing three presidents and sending hundreds of legislators to Washington, and despite influencing public policy with blizzards of mail and armies of lobbyists, evangelicals cannot point to a transformed America. As Charles Colson recently wrote in *Christianity Today*, "Belief in the Bible has declined and religious influence has been so thoroughly scrubbed from public life that any honest observer would have to regard this as a post-Christian culture. Gallup reports the most bewildering paradox: religion up, morality down. . . . We've protected our enterprises but in the process lost the culture."*

God's people everywhere should cry to the Lord in the words of the psalmist: "Wilt thou not revive us again: that thy people may rejoice in thee?" (Psalm 85:6, KJV). Revival is actually our only hope. But will the awakening come? Is there any real hope? What can we who seek God's best do to foster such a phenomenon? What does God expect of His people? If we can discover *how* God reveals himself in reviving times, it should aid us in answering these central issues and thus profoundly move us to seek a fresh touch from heaven. God *does* dramatically reveal himself in revival times, and He always discloses himself according to His essential attributes as *Father, Sovereign, Hope, Holy, Grace, Power, Love, and Availability*. The very nature of God revealing himself demonstrates the need and essence of a

---

*"National and International Religion Report," Stephen M. Wike, Publisher, Roanoke, VA.

true revival today. Simply put, we need to see and experience God afresh and anew.

Conclusion

The theme text of this biblical search, the often-quoted 2 Chronicles 7:14, epitomizes all that can be said concerning God's disclosure of himself in spiritual awakening. Moreover, the text not only unveils God for who He is, it explicitly shows His people how to respond in the light of His revealed nature. Actually, the revelation of God is the beginning of renewal, for as God declares himself, a commensurate response is immediately elicited from believers. This basic essential principle— revelation and response—becomes the framework of this study on spiritual awakenings.

The well-known theme verse is embedded in the dynamic story of Solomon's dedication of the temple. The beautiful promises of the theme text always resonate in the hearts of those who long to see revival: "If my people, who are called by my name, will humble themselves and pray and seek my face and turn from their wicked ways, *then I will hear from heaven and will forgive their sin and will heal their land*" (2 Chronicles 7:14). The various elements of this key verse become the thrust for all the accounts of biblical revivals that will unfold in this book. Thus to the Word of God we turn, clinging to our Lord's promise: "If my people . . . will . . . then *I will*."

The King Is Dead . . . Long Live the King

In a Spiritual Awakening God Reveals Himself as a

FATHER

Therefore, "His People, Called by His Name" Must Respond.
2 CHRONICLES 34:1–33; 35:1–19

Introduction

King Amon of Israel was dead, and a more wicked king Israel had rarely seen. Sin and debauchery abounded. Israel teetered on the brink of national disaster. Amon's son, Josiah, only eight years old, ascended the throne—just a stripling of a lad. Hope faded. Could God possibly be in all this? The answer is an emphatic *yes,* for God is Israel's *Father.* God, a *Father?* What an overwhelming thought! The mighty, sovereign Lord, a loving Father? Again, the question demands an emphatic *yes!* Hear His wonderful promise: "I will be a Father to you, and you will be my sons and daughters, says the Lord Almighty" (2 Corinthians 6:18; cf. Isaiah 43:6). It staggers the imagination. Perhaps there is hope after all! If Israel can experience God's fatherly presence, renewal may yet come. After all, they are "His people."

Early eighteenth-century Britain, much like Israel of old during the early days of the reign of "good King Josiah," languished for the Father's gracious presence among them. Although God had sent great revival during the seventeenth century, the nation had seemingly forgotten all about the Father's loving care. Consequently, the people were thrust into dire straits. Spiritual gloom, like a fog, had settled over the entire land. True, they had known the "glory days" when it almost seemed like their country was "full of the knowledge of the LORD as the waters cover the sea" (Isaiah 11:9). In the dramatic sixteen-hundreds, God as Father had been very real to them. The Puritan-Pietistic movement of those days had carried in its train a marvelous spiritual awakening. The Puritan-Pietists brought a time of refreshing to all of Europe. In that mighty revival, the British Isles had been particularly blessed. Because of its spiritual impact, the movement warrants a close look. It dramatically demonstrates, in more contemporary terms, how God reveals himself as a gracious Father and thus revives His people as they respond to His self-revelation.

The Puritan-Pietistic Awakening

The Puritan-Pietistic movement burst on the seventeenth-century scene as the church found itself in a depersonalizing vise-like grip of an inordinate quest for theological orthodoxy. As a consequence of this unbalanced approach of seeking detailed doctrine, many Reformation leaders and theologians of Europe lost contact with the practical and personal concerns of daily life. Concentrating their efforts on answering questions no longer being asked and solving problems the average person no longer had, the churches simply lost touch with the workaday world. So concerned for theological detail, they virtually forgot to project, at least in practical ways, the central truth that Luther had learned so well: "The just shall live by faith." The preachers and pastors simply got lost in a maze of theological minutiae. Under these circumstances, a disturbing number of nominal professing believers—who could not care less about theological minutiae—viewed their churches with unconcerned neglect. They saw them merely as institutions where one could be baptized, married, and buried. A contemporary quip points out that all the European State Church did for an apathetic people in christening babies, marrying, and burying people, was to "hatch, match, and dispatch" them. An ivory tower theological mentality had turned the church in on itself, isolating it from the real world. "Protestant scholasticism," as historians call the phenomenon, had won the day, and spiritual stagnation settled in. The pressing needs of people were left untouched, and the average person suffered alone.

What a tragedy! And it happened almost immediately after the great reformers—Calvin, Luther, Zwingli, Knox, and others—had accomplished their monumental work. How spiritually cold the churches had become in so short a time is all but unbelievable.

Then, just when it seemed a "protestant dark age" was about to descend on Europe, the Renaissance notwithstanding, there flashed a brilliant bolt of spiritual lightning on the dismal scene. Thousands were suddenly dazzled by the blinding light of God's reviving presence. Lutherans, Calvinists, Zwinglians, Anglicans, Baptists, and Armenians began to cry, "Father, I want to know you truly and *personally*." God heard the cry and a great revival burst on the scene. A profound spiritual movement began to take shape. God revealed himself as Father, awakening "His people."

Revival always begins in this fashion: God's *own people* being dramatically renewed when they grasp God as a Father—as our theme text emphasizes.

The evangelical awakening began to demonstrate its early, essential characteristics within English Calvinistic Puritanism. The Puritans preached God as the sovereign Father; and His people responded. The "glory days" returned and the great seventeenth-century awakening came about through the fervency of these Puritan-Pietists. As unkind to the movement as some undiscerning historians have been, they were great revival times.

To pinpoint the prime patriarch of the Puritan Revival is rather difficult. The spiritual roots of the new movement go deep into medieval mysticism. Nonetheless, many writers start with the sixteenth-century preacher-professor, William Perkins (1558–1603) of Warwickshire, England. He is often credited with being the progenitor of the pious. Perkins certainly epitomized the spirit of the movement. But there were other great men of God in the movement as well, men like John Hooper of Somerset. He, too, was certainly one of the "morning stars" in the awakening, as was Arthur Hildersham. Regardless of whom we deem as the beginner, it must be granted that a new spirit of revival had dawned like the morning sunrise on the British religious scene. Then something of a dramatic and widespread "chain reaction" of revival influence was set in motion, beginning with Perkins and the early Puritans in England. Revivals often tend to spread in a domino-like fashion.

The new spirit of revival soon crossed the English Channel through men like William Aimes, a student of Perkins, and invaded the Dutch Reformed churches of the seventeenth century. These Dutch Pietists in turn moved north and began to influence Lutheranism through spiritual giants like John

23

Arndt. As the eighteenth century was ushered in, the spirit of the awakening impacted vast areas of the Continent and touched men of God such as Phillip Spener, Herman Francke, Count Zinzendorf, Bengel, and their followers.

Before long, what historians call "a floodtide of godliness" swept over Europe. On the British scene, John Doanne, Daniel Dyke, John Smith, and a host of others arose. The spiritual superstars of the thrust were Richard Baxter, the epitome of Puritan-Pietism, John Bunyan of the mighty pen, Jeremy Taylor, and others. All were godly men endowed with powerful ministries.

But the movement, like all such movements, spent its force, and spiritual sterility once again set in. The inevitable recoil came. Europe bogged down in a spiritual "slough of despond." The early decades of the eighteenth century saw sin, sensuality, and crime rush in like a flood. England especially suffered. Then God did it again; as a gracious Father, He mightily revived His people. The new impetus of the evangelical spirit came through the mighty ministry of John and Charles Wesley and George Whitefield.*

The early germination of the Eighteenth-Century Revival had its conception in a smaller awakening that began in Saxony, Germany. On the estate of Count Ludwig von Zinzendorf, God as Father graciously poured out His Spirit, and a movement sprang forth that came to be known as the Moravian Revival.

The role played by the pietistic Moravians in the Wesleyan-Whitefield drama is well known. The Moravian testimony directly precipitated John Wesley's famous "Aldersgate" experience. Wesley first became open to the Moravian Brethren, on his voyage to America, when he saw the peace and calmness of the Brethren on the storm-tossed ship bound for Georgia. Later, in America, the following interview took place between John and the Moravian bishop, Professor Spangenberg of Jena:

Spangenberg: "Do you know Jesus Christ?"
Wesley: "I know He is the Savior of the World."

---

*George Whitefield sailed the Atlantic seven times and was used powerfully by God to spread America's "First Great Awakening." American greats like Jonathan Edwards arose in that context.

Spangenberg: "True, but do you know that he has saved you?"

Wesley: "I hope He has died to save me."

Spangenberg (later): "I fear they were vain words."

After Wesley's so-called "failure" in Georgia, he returned to England only to pen in his journal, "I went to America to convert the heathen, but, oh, who will convert me?" Back in London, Peter Bohler, another Moravian, crossed the Wesley brothers' path. He helped both John and brother Charles tremendously.* Charles soon found a confident faith in Christ. Then, three days later, John recorded in his journal:

Wednesday, May 24, 1738. In the evening I went very unwillingly to the Society in Aldersgate Street, where one was reading Luther's preface to the Epistle to the Romans. About a quarter before nine, while he was describing the change wrought by God in the heart through faith in Christ, I felt my heart strangely warmed. I felt I did trust Christ, Christ alone, for salvation; and an assurance was given me that He had taken away my sins, even mine, and saved me from the law of sin and death.[1]

Seven months later, early on New Year's morning, 1739, along with some Moravian Brethren, the significant Fetter Lane "Little Pentecost" occurred. Wesley described the stirring scene in his journal:

Mr. Hall, Kinchin, Ingham, Whitefield, Hutchins, and my brother, Charles, were present at our love feast in Fetter Lane, with about sixty of our brethren. About three in the morning, as we were continuing instant in prayer, the power of God came mightily upon us, insomuch that many cried out for exceeding joy, and many fell to the ground. As soon as we were recovered a little from that awe and amazement at the presence of His Majesty, we broke out with one voice, "We praise Thee, O God; we acknowledge Thee to be the Lord."[2]

The Eighteenth-Century Awakening had dawned.

---

*It is important to the history of the revival to understand that George Whitefield had been converted two years earlier. He was preaching with great power to tens of thousands. Actually, he is the real father of Methodism. (See Arnold Dallimore's work on George Whitefield, *Banner of Truth Trust*.)

George Whitefield, Wesley's close friend, had been preaching with tremendous effect two years before the Wesleys were converted. But now George, John, and Charles joined hearts and hands, and the movement was launched that historians contend saved England from a fate similar to the devastating French Revolution.

God the Father blessed His people in the Great Awakening of the eighteenth century. Actually the Puritan-Pietistic awakening gave birth to modern evangelicalism. But that is how it always is in a true spiritual revival. God reveals himself as Father and consequently, first of all, revives His own people. Those faithful Europeans responded to His fatherly grace, and the fog lifted. The gloom dissipated, and the "sun of righteousness" dawned. Revival had come.

Such was the need of Israel many centuries earlier. How well young King Josiah realized that reality!

The Revival Under Josiah

The Puritan movement, culminating in the Wesley-Whitefield Revival, stands as a dramatic illustration of the sort of awakening that occurred during the seventh-century B.C. reign of King Josiah, recorded in 2 Chronicles, chapters 35–36. The Josiah revival, as true of the eighteenth-century awakening, boasts all the earmarks of a great awakening wherein God shows His fatherly care for His children and thus quickens them as they respond to that loving care.

Israel's Need

Israel was desperate. It had been years, many years, since God had significantly blessed His chosen people. "Oh, that a true movement of the Lord's free grace would come upon us!" cried many a burdened Israelite. Was not God their Father? Were they not His people? Would He not revive them? Surely He would. He is always faithful; so they began to respond and cry out to their Father God. But it proved a long, difficult journey to the goal of a true spiritual awakening for the Israelites. Everything seemed pitted against a real revival.

Many years had come and gone since any significant spiritual movement had surged through Israel. The land languished. Some of the Jews even wondered if they truly were "God's Chosen People." Two kings in succession had proved to be sinful, sensuous, self-serving rulers, and the nation had wandered after their wicked ways. The temple was virtually covered in dust; worship had all but died. The Book of the Law—God's Word—was lost. Idolatry reigned. The religious leaders corrupted and defiled themselves. They degenerated into mere hirelings. Intrigue, interest buying, plots, even murder dominated the court. Desperation and despair characterized the scene. Where was their Father God? Why did He not put a stop to all the moral decay and destruction?

Manasseh had been one of those evil Israelite kings of the Southern Kingdom that brought such despair to the land. He had rebuilt the high places (of idol worship) "which his father Hezekiah had broken down" and he "erected altars to the Baals and made Asherah poles" (2 Chronicles 33:3). Manasseh had even built pagan altars in the "temple of the LORD" (2 Chronicles 33:5). Incredible—actually erecting idolatrous altars in the courts of the Lord!

But the Father is so gracious; He granted a little refreshing to His people. In the last years of Manasseh's fifty-five-year reign, the king did come to his senses and effected some reform, but it was far too late. The reformation produced little impact on the people. Yet, it did shed a faint ray of hope for revival for the future. God as Father had not completely forsaken His children.

Manasseh's son Amon took the throne after his father's death and, if anything, outdid his father in corrupting the land. After ruling for only two years he was murdered. Then the fickle people rose up and killed the murderers. Intrigue infected all circles. The country sunk into the pits of spiritual debauchery, and sensible political and religious life virtually collapsed.

The wayward Israelites had been warned about such matters. God never leaves himself without a witness. Zephaniah, a contemporary prophet, had issued the call of alarm: " 'I will sweep away both men and animals; I will sweep away the birds of the air and the fish of the sea. The wicked will have only heaps of rubble when I cut off man from the face of the earth,' declares the LORD. 'I will stretch out my hand against Judah and against all who live in Jerusalem. I will cut off from this place every remnant of Baal, the names of the pagan and idolatrous priests' " (Zephaniah 1:3–4). Destruction seemed imminent.

But then, right in the midst of that dismal scenario of impending judgment, *the sovereign Father did something beautiful.* And it all began with the birth of a baby.

Josiah's Birth

The year was 656 B.C. when Josiah was born. Eight years later, the people made the small lad their king. They shouted: "The King is dead. . . . Long live the King." But could God work in that scenario? Josiah was only eight, and his father and grandfather had hardly been sterling examples of godliness. The people had settled down in their idolatry and sin and were enjoying it. Surely Zephaniah's word of impending judgment would be fulfilled.

In 642 B.C. the young boy ascended the throne. Then, just eight years later, we read of the first real hope for revival. At the age of sixteen Josiah "began to seek the God of his father David" (2 Chronicles 34:3). Why did this young man, encompassed by unbelievable circumstances, begin to seek the Lord? He certainly did not receive any inspiration from his predecessors Manasseh or Amon. His entire background and environment militated against any such seeking. Only the *sovereign grace of God* can explain it.

It must be said again that revival always finds its final answer in God's sovereignty. The Lord's people need to awaken to the reality that He alone controls His work and will give His people what they need when they need it. He is Lord of all—a truth easily forgotten in barren days, for in those times even God's people tend to become humanistic and secular. But He gives revival when and through whom He pleases. When God says this is the hour, *it is the hour.* His wisdom far outstrips ours, and He will always place the timing of awakenings in the divine economy of His plan. In sovereignty He does all things wisely and well. Josiah's revival is a shining example of this truth.

Of course, God's sovereign actions do not mean He never uses means. To the contrary, He always uses human instruments to accomplish His divine purpose. God does not work in a vacuum. A spiritual awakening invariably emanates out of God's sovereign grace *using human means.* Sadly, the church has carried on a heated debate over the paradox of divine sovereignty and human responsibility. It has at times even divided the church into rival factions.* But these two parallel truths run side by side in God's Word and must simply be accepted. On the horizon of heaven the two tracks will converge; until then we rest in faith and take God for how He reveals himself. He is sovereign and He uses human instruments in revival— *always.* That is how the Lord God has revealed himself and we are to yield humbly to that truth. After all, He is God, and His infinite wisdom can only be described in paradoxical terms.

In the Josiah revival, the Father's sovereign grace used the means of a young king. Josiah, by God's grace, came to know God as Lord and Father. Consequently, he responded properly and the awakening came.

The factors that actually precipitated Josiah's life-changing experience remain clouded by the dust of lost history. Nevertheless, we can speculate. The young king probably learned how his grandfather Manasseh had turned from idolatry in his last years. Perhaps the excesses of his father, Amon, disgusted his youthful idealism. The Book of the Law was not in hand, but surely some in the court knew something of God's Word, and may have shared it with the young man. Above all, we know that Zephaniah and other prophets were on the scene. Jeremiah, mighty man of God, surely dramatically impacted the situation. Some in the land did hear "Thus saith the LORD." Not only that, it must have been that somewhere someone was praying for God to visit His people again. A praying remnant can always be found in the formation of a nation born again. But regardless of what means God employed, Josiah proved to be a token of God's grace and came to know the Lord in such a fashion that he could be used in revival.

---

*This even occurred during the great Eighteenth-Century Revival. So-called "Calvinists" and "Armenians" battled over the issue, and it did damage to the awakening. It actually put Wesley and Whitefield, at least to an extent, in different camps.

In that context, Josiah made a wise decision; the Scriptures tell us he chose King David as his role model rather than his godless father and grandfather (2 Chronicles 34:2). The revival experienced its birth pangs almost immediately, even though Josiah was only twenty when the awakening commenced (2 Chronicles 34:3).

The Early Days of the Revival

The early days of the awakening moved forward on a pointed, two-pronged thrust. First, Josiah purged Judah and Jerusalem of its idols, its "high places, Asherah poles, carved idols and cast images" (2 Chronicles 34:3). Then, after purification from the pollution of idols, he launched a drive to involve all the people in repairing the Jerusalem temple. True worship of the Father was restored. In any age, idols must go, and genuine worship of the Father must be instituted. That always forms the initial steps in a true awakening.

Josiah personally carried out the destruction of the idols. By his own hand, he broke down the incense altars and dashed in pieces the graven images. The zealous young king had a true heart for God. Old Testament scholar Walter C. Kaiser makes an interesting observation here:

> Josiah also burned the dead bones of the false priests on their altars. By means of this action, Josiah apparently unwittingly fulfilled the prophecy of the man of God from Judah who had pronounced judgment against wicked Jeroboam for his idolatrous altar: "And the man cried against the altar by the word of the LORD, and said, 'O altar, altar,' thus says the LORD: 'Behold, a son shall be born to the house of David, Josiah by name; and he shall sacrifice upon you the priests of the high places who burn incense upon you, and men's bones shall be burned upon you' " (1 Kings 13:2). That was shortly after 931 B.C. Its fulfillment occurred some three hundred years later in 628 B.C. Yet, in this magnificent prophecy are included the name of the king, his act of discovering the bones of these desecrates, and the rebuke for this golden calf installation in the northern kingdom by a Davidic king.[3]

The purity of Josiah's own life demanded purity in the land.

It hardly needs be said there has never been a revival without a purge of that which pollutes and degenerates peoples and lands. The Holy Spirit, the Author of revival, is sensitive and readily grieved by sin, especially in the lives of believers. God invariably breaks the hearts of His people over their personal sin and waywardness. Whatever stands between a believer and absolute surrender to the lordship of Jesus Christ must be confessed and forsaken. Therefore, a purging of every "idol" becomes the first work of the Spirit in awakening His people. History constantly attests to this primary principle. A classic case in point is the Shantung Revival of 1927 in China.

Bertha Smith, Baptist missionary to China and Taiwan, became one of God's significant instruments in the great Shantung awakening. She often shared a personal story that illustrates the revival purification principle perfectly. Her testimony begins by relating that the Baptist missionaries serving in Shantung, the large northeast province of China, had all gathered at the seaport of Chefoo. Serious political unrest had precipitated the move. Days of uncertainty and confusion pervaded the compound. The faithful band of God's servants began to devote themselves to prayer, and God began to stir deeply among them. But Miss Smith must tell her own story:

> One of our number, Mrs. Charles Culpepper, Sr., had suffered much from optical neuritis, which had left only partial vision in the eye affected. A few months before we were called to Chefoo, the good eye began to cause trouble. The mission doctor in Laichowfu advised her to go to Peking for treatment.
>
> The Culpepper family went to Union Medical College Hospital. Due to the philanthropy of John D. Rockefeller, Jr., the world's best specialists were to be found there. The eye specialist at that time was from Vienna, Austria. He changed her glasses but gave no encouragement about an improvement in the general condition of her eyes.
>
> During those days in Chefoo when we often had fellowship . . . and heard . . . how God had marvelously healed all sorts of diseases, Mrs. Culpepper started having eye trouble again. There was still no eye specialist nearer than Peking, which was over 200 miles away. She did not believe he could do much for her, even if she could receive his care. She truly felt discouraged.

One evening the thought came to her to ask the prayer group to pray that the Lord would heal her. It was a very difficult thing to bring herself to do, for she still had the prejudice that had been in her mind for years concerning faith healing.

Since praying for the sick to be divinely healed had never been in her way of belief or practice, Mrs. Culpepper had never studied the Bible from this viewpoint. It was really the work of the Spirit during those days that brought her life before her like a movie. She began to see her real self as God saw her. Only the power of the Holy Spirit could have given her strength to talk very frankly with her husband, confessing sins against him and others. Even greater courage was given her to say to the whole group that she was most unworthy to be one of their number.

When the day agreed on arrived, twelve were present in the prayer meeting. Dr. Culpepper read from the fifth chapter of James: "Therefore confess your sins to one another, and pray for one another, that you may be healed. The prayer of a righteous man has great power in its effects" (James 5:16). He did not try to explain it; he was not leaving out anything of which the Bible spoke. He then put some olive oil on Mrs. Culpepper's head and asked all to come up and lay their hands on her head and pray.

I had gone into that room, so far as I knew, absolutely right with the Lord. I would not have dared to go otherwise. But when I stretched my hand out to Mrs. Culpepper's head, I had to bring it back. There stood facing me a missionary with whom there had been a little trouble. In her early years she had been head of a girls' school, but for several years she had been teaching illiterate women to read.

I had been asked to serve as principal in our boys' school in Chefoo while the missionary principal was on furlough. I had majored in education, and by that time had ten years' experience in teaching and thought I was "the last word" in education! I had recommended Miss Hartwell to lead daily worship in that school. After a few weeks, I asked another missionary to tell her that methods for teaching old women were not appropriate for high school boys. She was hurt, of course. But what about my proud self? I did not have a particle of sympathy for her. Right there before everyone, I had to say, "Miss Hartwell, I did not have the proper attitude toward you about that school affair. I beg you to forgive me!" My hand then joined the others and we prayed.

Had I refused to confess that sin, and joined in the prayer with it covered, I believe that I would have hindered the prayer of the others, and the eye could not have been healed.

Because all were right with God and of one heart, heaven came down! We did not have to wait to see whether or not Mrs. Culpepper's eye was healed! We knew in our hearts that she would never have another attack.

Walking around the room rejoicing and praising the Lord, we were all on a mountaintop of ecstasy. Then I had to be the joykiller. There came over me such a sense of our inconsistency, that I had to speak of it.

"What kind of missionaries are we?" I asked. We had gone through a week of heart searching, humbling ourselves before each other and before the Lord, in order that we might be altogether right with him, so that he could hear our prayers and heal the physical eye of one of our own number. Yet we had never gone to this much self negation for preparation to pray for the opening of the spiritual eyes of the Chinese to whom we had been sent. Our mountaintop of ecstasy suddenly became a valley of humiliation. We all went to our knees in contrite confession for having been so careless as to have gone along supposing that we were right with the Lord, while holding all kinds of attitudes that could have kept the Lord's living water from flowing through, out to the Chinese.

Within a few weeks we were able to return to our various posts of work. Everyone went back to teaching and preaching the tragedy of sin in the life and heart of a Christian.[4]

This graphic story of Bertha Smith propels us right into the heart of the primary issue: Before a deep awakening comes, *all idols must go.* In one sense, that is a revival itself, for only then the Father God will "forgive their sin and will heal the land."

Worship in Revival

After purification comes acceptable worship. So King Josiah set about repairing the temple (2 Chronicles 34:8). The Jerusalem temple had not heard the praise of God the Father for at least seventy-five years. It was crumbling into a sad state of disrepair. The attacking armies of the Assyrians had badly damaged it. God's people demonstrated little heart to repair it;

they found their new idols sufficient, that is, until revival came. Remember, God the Father first revives His people, and they are to respond in genuine worship from a pure heart. Jesus said, "God is a Spirit: and they that worship him must worship him in Spirit and in truth" (John 4:24, KJV). Further, Paul tells us what the nature of real worship is: "I appeal to you therefore, brethren, by the mercies of God, to present your bodies as a living sacrifice, holy and acceptable to God, which is your spiritual worship" (Romans 12:1, RSV). Worship of the Father "in Spirit and in truth" finds its fulfillment in complete surrender to His will. That becomes a foundational principle in any spiritual awakening. God's people become yielded—totally yielded—to God. So King Josiah gave himself to lifting up the standard of obedience to the will of God's law and instituted true worship of the true God among true yielded believers.

A strange cluster of circumstances set itself up at that point; the priests received a commission to raise the money for the repairs, but they grew dilatory in using the funds to effect the actual reconstruction. Josiah demanded an accounting: "Why are you not repairing the house? Now therefore take no more money from your acquaintances, but hand it over for the repair of the house" (2 Kings 12:7, RSV). Again, the zeal of good King Josiah surfaced. *Prompt* obedience to God's will is essential. Evan Roberts, God's key instrument in the Welsh Revival of 1904–1906, admonished believers to "obey the Spirit *promptly*." That word did much to open the floodgates of revival blessings on Wales in 1904.

With that same word of King Josiah, the repairs got under way—this time through the leadership of faithful laymen. God uses anyone who will do His will, clergy or laity alike. God sees no real difference regarding responsibility to perform His will and purpose. Revival moves forward on the dedication of *yielded* people, regardless of their role in the life of the church.

Then the Father did something most gracious for His children: "While they were bringing out the money that had been taken into the temple of the LORD, Hilkiah the priest found the Book of the Law of the LORD that had been given through Moses" (2 Chronicles 34:14). The Law, God's Word, at last recovered! But what a situation! It is hard to imagine that the Father's people would lose God's own Word and then not diligently seek it. Such indifference proved the depth of their spiritual apathy and unconcern before the awakening. But God's reviving, sovereign grace can reach down to the very depths of apathy. Therefore, the Father saw to it that His Word would come alive once more to the multitudes. Hilkiah gave the book to Shaphan, the king's servant, and he in turn read it to Josiah, and the King then eagerly gave it to all the people. With the Word of God finally found and heard, the people set their hearts to obey, and an immediate revival explosion resounded over the land.

The Power of the Bible in Revival

A spiritual awakening always soars on the wings of the Word. No matter how long people neglect the truth of God, one day it will surface and accomplish its wonder work. Thus, when the young king heard the Scriptures, he sat spellbound. If the rediscovered Law were the book of Deuteronomy, it would have taken two or three hours to hear it all. If it were the entire Pentateuch, the first five books of the Bible the Jews called the Law, it would have consumed twelve hours. Imagine King Josiah sitting enthralled through it all. Who today would sit spellbound for hours just listening to the Old Testament Law being read in the light of our seeming superficial quest for "instant spirituality"? But such is the captivating power of God's Word when it comes in the power of the Holy Spirit: "When this king heard the words of the law he rent his clothes" (2 Chronicles 34:19, RSV). Verse 27 tells us the king wept. In a word, Josiah deeply *repented*. He was a godly king; yet, when he saw his life in the light of the Scriptures, he deeply and profoundly repented. The Word had searched him through and through. As always in revival, God broke his heart over personal sin. He said, "Go, inquire of the LORD for me and for those who are left in Israel and in Judah, concerning the words of the book that has been found; for great is the wrath of the LORD that is poured out on us, because our fathers have not kept the word of the LORD, to do according to all that is written in this book" (2 Chronicles 34:21, RSV). The rediscovery of the Law proved a far greater blessing than the mere repairing of the temple building. Now worship could emanate from a pure, yielded life—a life lived in accordance with God's truth. Surrender to God supercedes sanctuaries in which to worship God. Actually, the discovery of the Word of God marked the beginning of the revival in its most profound depth.

After the king heard the Word he sought out Huldah the prophetess. This woman of God spoke in the Spirit, warning the court of impending judgment. Her word of warning deeply moved the king. God uses women in revival as well as men. The king then called for a "solemn assembly." He gathered "all the people both great and small; and he read in their hearing all the words of the book of the covenant which had been found in the house of the LORD" (2 Chronicles 34:30, RSV). What a dramatic scene it must have been. There were priests and Levites standing before the people as God's representatives. The elders were there too—those leaders highly respected by the populace. And before them all stood King Josiah, God's repentant, revived ruler. In that tense setting the Word of God thundered forth.

As the Scriptures were read the people trembled. The heinousness of their sin in the light of God's revealed truth overwhelmed them. The Bible always pierces the heart and leads to confession—often open confession—and repentance. It truly is "sharper than any double-edged sword" (Hebrews 4:12). It cuts, and then heals as it moves people Godward. "Solemn assemblies" in the Bible focus on the Bible. In that context, God works mightily.

The power of the Scriptures will invariably impact needy people and places. History is replete with this principle. Back in 1481, a depressed, disturbed Roman Catholic monk of the Dominican Order immersed himself in the Word of God. The Scriptures dramatically transformed his life. He began to preach the Word in the magnificent St. Mark's Cathedral of Florence, Italy. The truth of God's Word came with such power that the entire city of Florence was revolutionized, just like Israel under Josiah. A great spiritual awakening invaded every vestige of northern Italy. Hardly a home escaped untouched. Florence itself glowed with the glory of God. The results of the so-called Florentine Revival were magnificent. A powerful story unfolds in that awakening, perfectly illustrating the power of the Word.

The Florentine Revival

Italy writhed in turmoil as the fifteenth century dawned. Economically the feudal system was rapidly collapsing, leaving a serious social and economic vacuum. Consequently, a new move to political centralization and urbanization began. As the cities grew they became a variable squalor. Out of the cultural chaos, materialism commenced its dominant rise. In the midst of it all, Italy blazed with the Renaissance. The intellectual gloom and depression of the past one thousand years was burning off like intellectual fog in the hot rising sun of rationalism. Philosophers were reviving the thought of ancient Greece. The printing press had just been invented, placing books in previously empty hands. Constantinople had fallen to the barbarous Turks, and the scholars fled, spreading all over Italy, fashioning the peninsula of city states into the radiating center of the breaking Enlightenment. A new day dawned, but it became an increasing secular one. Could the church rise to the revolutionary challenge? Many doubted it could—the odds seemed just too great.

The Roman Church itself afforded little hope; for years it had been eroding at its very foundations. Over 200 years had slipped away since the great revival under St. Francis of Assisi had breathed new life into the church—now the breath was gone. The popes scandalized Europe. Pope Sextus IV was known for his cruelty, Alexander VI for his "unnatural" passion, and Julius II for his infidelities. The Vatican had even planned the murder of political leader Lorenzo de Medici of Florence. The pope's nephew planned it and an archbishop attempted to carry it out. The one actually murdered turned out to be Lorenzo's brother who was a Roman priest. The murderers were then executed. After that, as unbelievable as it seems, Rome issued a bill of excommunication against the executioners—and the church had arranged it all! The corruption of Rome sent a putrid odor to the heavens. Even Machiavelli said, "To the church and priests of Rome we Italians owe this obligation—that we have become void of religion and corrupt."

A righteous voice was desperately needed. God sent that voice in the person of a depressed monk of the Dominican Order: Savonarola of Florence. Born September 21, 1452 in Ferrara,

Savonarola felt the call of God early in life. In April of 1475 he entered the Dominican monastery in Bologna. There he devoted himself to a study of the Scriptures. Light began to filter into his tradition-saturated soul. After a long, agonizing spiritual struggle, Friar Savonarola came to a firm grasp of the essential Gospel. He came to Christ in salvation. Actually, he became a pre-Reformation reformer.

In 1481, Savonarola was sent to Florence to the Monastery of St. Mark. In that setting the prophecies of the book of Revelation came alive to the young monk. He began fasting and praying night and day as he pored over the Bible.

During that time the revived monk received an appointment as the parish preacher in St. Mark's Cathedral. The last book of the Bible became his sermonic text. He preached over 300 sermons on the book of Revelation. He pronounced judgment on the entire corrupt cultural milieu of his day. He struck out at the vices that engulfed the city. He dragged into light the scandalous sins of the country. He became a fearless, incorruptible prophet. He passionately cried out for repentance. "Christ alone is the answer," he heralded. An avalanche of grace poured forth from the altar of the Father, and Florence was turned upside down. A revival had come. One historian described those days and Savonarola's spiritual impact:

> So large was the concourse gathered to hear him that he had to transfer himself to the Cathedral. Here, day after day, the population of Florence thronged to see and hear him. Many were drawn by curiosity, but even the most superficial became awed as they listened to the burning words of the preacher. The crowds thronged and pressed each other so close that there was hardly room to breathe; they built seats against the walls in the front of an amphitheater, and still the space was insufficient.
>
> And how is it possible at this date to describe the preacher? The deep, resonant voice, the flash of his deep-set, penetrating eyes, the impassioned gestures, the marvelous flow of his oratory as, swept along with the fiery vehemence of his great soul, he discoursed to men of the eternal verities, of the awful facts of death and judgment to come? First he would begin in measured and tranquil tones, taking up the subject, turning it quietly 'round, suggesting some scholarly exposition, advancing some inter-

pretation, dealing with it casually, critically, suggestively; then, suddenly, often without warning, he would change, the meditative style was flung aside as the mantle of the prophet fell upon him; fire flashed from his eyes, the thunder came into his voice; now in passionate entreaty, now in scorching indignation, the sentences rushed out, never halting, never losing intensity or volume, but growing and growing until his voice became as the voice of God himself, and all the building rocked and swayed as if it moved to the mighty passion of his words.

And what of the hearers? They were as clay in his hands. Tears gushed from their eyes, they beat their breasts, they cried unto God for mercy, the church echoed and re-echoed with their sobs. Those who report his sermons suddenly break off and add: "Here was I so overcome with weeping that I could not go on." Pico della Mirandola, one of the most learned men of the day, says that the mere sound of Savonarola's voice was as the clap of doom; a cold shiver ran through the marrow of his bones, the hairs of his head stood on end as he listened. Another tells that these sermons caused such terror, alarm, such sobbing and tears, that every one passed through the streets without speaking, more dead than alive.[5]

That is revival preaching of the Word. The city of Florence virtually became the "City of God." Someone expressed it in these words: "The carnival seemed like Lent."

Savonarola thundered against the corruption of the church as well as the evils of the Florentines. Rome would not long tolerate that, and soon a bull from the Vatican sped its way to St. Mark's. The pope said the monk must die, "even if he be another John the Baptist." With its vicious tentacles reaching out, the church engulfed him. On May 23, 1499, Savonarola was led to Prazza della Signora, along with two friends, Friar Domenico and Friar Silvester. The gallows awaited. The gibbet, to the awe of the huge crowd that had gathered, was silhouetted against the gray sky in the form of a cross. When Savonarola saw the scene he said, "The Lord hath suffered as much for me." The noose was placed around his neck. The Bishop said, "I separate you from the Church militant and from the Church triumphant." The brave martyr replied, "Not from the church triumphant, that is beyond thy power." The rope jerked and the man of God joined the church triumphant.

Savonarola was gone. But the *truth* that he had so powerfully spoken to the people remained, and thus the revival lived on in many lives and did much to pave the way for the great awakening we call the Reformation. Out of death sprang abundant life.

That is the very thing God did for Israel under Josiah when the Word came home to their hearts. Sin was exposed and the people repented. That is revival. As a Father, God was reviving His people. And as they should, they began to respond.

The Covenant of Revival

After the power of the Word had done its convicting, judging work, Israel made a new covenant commitment (2 Chronicles 34:21). Josiah, before the people and for the people, entered into a covenant with the Lord God to *obey* all the words of the Book. One must do more than *hear* the Word to be revived, one must *do* the Word (James 1:22). In the Josiah revival, God so moved upon the people that "the inhabitants of Jerusalem did according to the covenant of God, the God of their fathers" (2 Chronicles 34:32, RSV). That constitutes a *true* spiritual awakening.

The Results of the Awakening

But did the revival last? Did it prove more than just an emotional outburst or a quest for the relaying of old conservative foundations? The Bible says, "As long as he [Josiah] lived, they [the people] did not fail to follow the LORD, the God of their fathers" (2 Chronicles 34:33). It did last, and it carried the people on in true obedience to the will of God as revealed in the Scriptures. Revived people keep the covenant. Real revival endures the trials of time.

Not only do awakenings continue, they normally deepen. In Israel, even further reforms were effected after the people were enlightened by the Law. As one put it, "Certain practices which formerly did not appear bad now stood out as sickening to God and to the sober minded."[6] That is the process the New Testament knows as *progressive sanctification*. Revival sensitizes God's awakened people and then continually deepens their sanctification, that is, the purifying of their lives. The response to the reviving Father always manifests itself in a deepening experience. Illustrations of that principle abound during revival times.

As a case in point, I was once preaching in a small church when the conviction of the Holy Spirit fell in power and mightily revived several of the believers. One night, during an after-service prayer meeting, the convicting, sanctifying Holy Spirit plowed deep in many lives. One brokenhearted teenage girl began to sob out her prayer: "Dear Lord, I'm so sorry. I ask you to forgive me for stealing." She went on in her prayer, "Lord, it was just a salt shaker I took from that restaurant where we kids went after the ball game to celebrate. We were just having a good time, and I stole the salt shaker as a memento of the game—but, Lord, I'm so sorry. Please forgive me! I'll take it back if I can remember where it was. Please forgive me." Her heart was crushed.

We can easily retort, "Is that not taking it all a bit too far?" Not really! Stealing is stealing, be it a thousand grains of salt or a thousand dollars. The Holy Spirit is most sensitive to sin in His saints, and those whom He awakens He likewise sensitizes. This has been made abundantly clear. The revived life is a life of constant discovery of areas of one's experience to be confessed and plunged under the blood of Christ and yielded up to the covenant-keeping Father God. That sort of response on the part of God's own people deepens and extends and perpetuates a great awakening.

Keeping the Passover: Redemption in Revival

After the hearing and heeding of the Law, the confession of sin, and the reestablishment of the covenant, Josiah then celebrated the Passover. That significant move took place in the eighteenth year of his reign. The Passover, of course, spoke of God's redemption. Let it be stressed, there is *never* a genuine spiritual awakening that does not result in redemption—redemption in the broadest sense of the word. If a real revival breaks across any land, multitudes will be converted to Christ, and civic and social righteousness will come in like a flood. Effective evangelization and social rectitude are perennially

41

the products of a powerful awakening. It has always been so, and always shall be. Any movement that does not result in evangelism and social change, regardless of how exciting or emotional or captivating it may be, does not stem from God, or at least has not moved to the point God intends it to move. God is interested in redeeming the lost and purifying social corruption. He is a loving Father and He wants to "heal the land" as well as save the lost.

So, God kept His revival promise to His people that He had made through the prophet Zephaniah: "The LORD, your God, is in your midst, a warrior who gives victory; he will rejoice over you with gladness, he will renew you in his love" (Zephaniah 3:17, RSV). He is a gracious Father who constantly revives His people—His people of any hour or era. Thus, He stands in our contemporary "midst" as a "warrior" to give us the "victory" we so desperately need.

Conclusion

Several significant revival principles surface in the spiritual awakening under Josiah. First, the constant need for revival is pointed up. The human heart is decidedly prone to wander from God. People stray, even God's people. And with that wandering, moral decay and erosions soon follow in the church and society as a whole. Actually, a viable culture cannot long endure without periodical awakenings. Nor can the church stand unless regularly revived. But the Father loves His world and longs to send revival and draw all people to himself.

Secondly, the Word of God becomes central in all great awakenings. The Josiah revival makes this abundantly clear. When the Bible was read, sin was revealed and Israel turned back to God. Furthermore, the continuing history of revivals constantly attests to that, as the Florentine Revival illustrates. The powerful biblical preaching and teaching of men like Jonathan Edwards, George Whitefield, the Tennets, and others put real bite into America's First Great Awakening. It is a return to the Word of God that rests at the heart of any revival; actually, that is what makes an awakening last.

Thirdly, as now clearly seen, revival begins as God reveals His essential attributes and character as a loving Father to His own people. *And they must respond.* If an awakening is to dawn over the land, its first rays must break in on God's own covenant people, and they are to react positively to the Spirit's prompting. This truth shall be seen many times over as this examination of scriptural awakenings continues. In the final analysis, an awakening begins or ends on the basis of how believers respond to the Father's revelation of himself. Therefore, as God unveils himself as a loving, reviving Father, God's people, those "called by His name," must respond in committal, repentance, worship, and service. That response becomes the point of it all, for that is revival.

Let My People Go

In a Spiritual Awakening God Reveals Himself as
SOVEREIGN

Therefore, "Humble Yourself."
EXODUS 1–3

Introduction

A study of God's Word makes it increasingly evident that in the great moments of spiritual awakening, God always reveals himself as the sovereign Lord. He is not only a gracious Father, He stands as the reigning King, as clearly implied in the Josiah revival. The Bible abounds in the central truth of God's *absolute sovereignty*. Deuteronomy 4:39 declares, "Know therefore this day, and lay it to your heart, that the Lord is God in heaven above and on the earth beneath; there is no other" (RSV). Throughout the entire scriptural revelation, God's almighty power and ultimate control of all things constantly surfaces:

> When Abram was ninety-nine years old the Lord appeared to Abram, and said to him, "I am God Almighty; walk before me and be blameless" (Genesis 17:1).
> For dominion belongs to the LORD and he rules over the nations (Psalm 22:28).
> For nothing is impossible with God (Luke 1:37).
> For who resists his will?" (Romans 9:19).
> Then I heard what sounded like a great multitude, like the roar of rushing waters and like loud peals of thunder, shouting: "Hallelujah! For our Lord God Almighty reigns" (Revelation 19:6).

Paul brings it all together calling Him the "blessed and only Sovereign, the King of kings and Lord of lords" (1 Timothy 6:15, RSV). This vital revival principle certainly manifested itself at the dedication of Solomon's Temple.

God's Promise and Place in Revival

When the sovereign Lord God spoke to Solomon on that dedication day, He gave the king a veritable multitude of fascinating and thrilling promises concerning spiritual awakening. As our theme text succinctly states, "If my people . . . will . . . then *I will*." But where we cause the interpretive accent to fall on this significant theme verse largely determines our essential understanding of God in revival, and thus our subsequent action. Through the years many of God's people who have responded to the Lord's promises with real revival concern have seemingly placed the emphasis on the phrase "if my people will." Perhaps because these words rest in the initial part of the verse, there has been a decided tendency to inject the revival emphasis into this first clause; thus stressing what appears to be the conditions believers must meet to receive God's best blessings. Moreover, we all tend to be such activists that we seem to believe we must always act before God will move. Consequently Christians are urged first and foremost to "humble themselves," "pray," "seek God's face," and "turn from their wicked ways." Only then, the exhortation goes, will revival come.

But is this interpretive emphasis the correct one? It is highly questionable. Laying the primary stress on what constitutes the human responsibilities in fulfilling the covenant of revival seems dubious. If one does not exercise extreme caution, such an emphasis can soon deteriorate into what has been called "evangelical humanism," that is, human activity in spiritual matters that appears evangelical in tone and language, but in the final analysis is really quite humanistic, nonetheless. Such an approach, if pushed too far, projects human activity as the primary key to revival, thus relegating God's actions and movings to a secondary, dependent position. This obviously attenuates God's divine sovereignty in spiritual awakenings. We must never slip into the spiritual syndrome of seeing God as some "Great Computer in the Sky" whom we can program by certain human activity, even evangelical actions, then push the "readout key" and expect an awakening automatically to emerge. Such an attitude not only misreads the thrust of the promises to Solomon, it can even thwart revival blessings. In all awakenings, God always stands as *Sovereign*. Actually, that attribute of the Most High constitutes the supreme principle of revival. He gives revival when He in His sovereign grace pleases. Spiritual awakening springs forth from God who alone is the emanating source of all true renewal. Seemingly, a forgotten axiom of spiritual blessings is: *"He* restoreth my soul" (Psalm 23:2, KJV).*

Moreover, a humanistic approach misses a very important principle in the revival promise of our theme text. Insisting that believers must "humble themselves, pray, seek God's face, and turn from their wicked way," implying that only then will God send a revival, misconstrues what actually constitutes a spiritual awakening. In a very real sense, when God's people profoundly "humble themselves, pray, seek God's face, and turn from their sins," *the spiritual awakening has in a significant sense already begun.* Strictly speaking, the spiritual disciplines of 2 Chronicles 7:14 are not just the conditions *for* a true revival; actually, *they are the revival itself.* That is what a spiritual awakening is, at least from the personal perspective among believers. Those spiritual disciplines are realized only when God in His sovereignty has already mightily moved on His own people and begun His reviving work. These conditions do not so much bring a revival to the church as *they are the revival itself.* Of course, God's sovereignty in revival does not mean God's people are not required to humble themselves, seek His face, pray, etc. It simply means the initial act in revival begins with God moving and enabling His people to do so. But when believers truly do respond, then God's promises are fulfilled and He will "hear from heaven and forgive their sin and heal their land." That constitutes the results of the awakening. When God's people permit God in sovereign grace to revive them, then He can work wonders in the whole land—saving, healing, restoring, and glorifying His name.

Therefore, a redressing is called for to strike the delicate balance in the paradox of divine sovereignty and human responsibility, never forgetting that in real revival the scriptural accent rests on God himself; the "I will" clause of 2 Chronicles 7:14. Crass, shallow activism produces little, if any, lasting re-

---

*This does not mean God uses no means in revival; nor does it mean we should not discipline ourselves and meet the personal spiritual challenges of 2 Chronicles 7:14. Those disciplines are always incumbent upon God's people as God's Spirit moves upon them. As G. Campbell Morgan once pointed out: "We cannot organize revival, but we can set our sails to catch the wind from Heaven when God chooses to blow upon His people once again." Quoted by Stephen F. Olford in, *Lord Open the Heavens* (Wheaton: Harold Shaw Publishers, 1962), p. 92.

sults. The time has come to humble ourselves under God's sovereign hand, forsake manipulative, fleshly activity, and focus on who God is and look to Him as the one true sovereign Source of genuine spiritual awakening.

However, when we do finally recognize God's sovereignty in awakening, we will become more active and involved in the human responsibilities for revival than ever before. The reason shines clear: We will see God for who He truly is, and that revelation elicits from sincere believers genuine humility and faith, just like the reaction of Isaiah when He saw the Lord high and lifted up and cried out, "Here am I, send me" (Isaiah 6:8, KJV).

Now, if that approach and understanding of our theme text can be accomplished theologically *and experientially,* we can begin to pray humbly and properly and trust God to act in His sovereign grace, sending a significant spiritual awakening.

The Need of the Day

Surely we should earnestly seek a fresh revival in our needy time! Sovereignty does not preclude seeking. Society seems on the move to masochistic madness. We must react. Think of the moral suicide the western world is committing! Not only that, most Christians are not even aware that America, for example, is the fourth most unbelieving nation on earth, exceeded only by Russia, China, and India. Only three countries surpass the United States in numbers of lost people. And in Europe only four or five percent of the population attend any church, while the secularized millions plunge on heedlessly to a land of eternal despair. And what about the unreached billions who know virtually nothing of the Gospel? That is not to mention the unconcern of the church. On both sides of the Atlantic and in both hemispheres, we can thank apathetic, preoccupied, proud Christians for the tragic situation society faces. But the sad state can be rectified by a real revival through a humbled, awakened people. The truth stands out in bold relief that revival dramatically transforms an entire nation. It has happened so many times throughout history.

The Frontier Revival

In May of 1801, frontier pastor Barton Stone called for a four-day special meeting at the little Cane Ridge Meeting House nestled away in the cane-breaks of Bourbon County, Kentucky. Stone, originally from the Carolinas, had been preaching at Cane Ridge in central Kentucky for some time. Urged to serve the small Kentucky country congregation by none other than the famous frontiersman Daniel Boone, the farmers of Bourbon County appreciated Stone's effective preaching. When the pastor issued the special call, many laid aside their plows and came to the May meeting at Cane Ridge. Blessings abounded. Stone called for a similar meeting again in August, and to the utter astonishment of all, historical United States Army records* state that over 20,000 people arrived for the four-day meeting. They literally had to send in the Army to help aid the vast throngs. Even if that figure got inflated by enthusiasm, it is amazing to think that thousands arrived to a little frontier church that could seat no more than 250 worshipers. God's great sovereign surprise had them aghast. It was an incredible event. Where all the people came from is still a mystery. Cane Ridge was still on the American frontier. Among the thousands converted at Cane Ridge was James B. Finley, who later became a Methodist circuit rider. He described the revival scene that had erupted:

The noise was like the roar of Niagara. The vast sea of human beings seemed to be agitated as if by a storm. I counted seven ministers, all preaching at one time, some on stumps, others in wagons, and one was standing on a tree which had, in falling, lodged against another. . . . Some of the people were singing, others praying, some crying for mercy in the most piteous accents, while others were shouting most vociferously. While witnessing these scenes, a peculiarly-strange sensation, such as I had never felt before, came over me. My heart beat tumultuously, my knees trembled, my lips quivered, and I felt as though I must fall to the ground. A strange supernatural power seemed to pervade the entire mass of mind there collected. . . . I stepped

---

*Stone and other leaders of the revival had to call in the Army to help in managing the multitudes that came. The records are actual official Army estimates.

up on to the log, where I could have a better view of the surging sea of humanity. At one time I saw at least five hundred swept down in a moment, as if a battery of a thousand guns had been opened upon them, and then immediately followed shrieks and shouts that rent the very heavens.[1]

Soon the entire central American frontier blazed with revival. The Presbyterians and Methodists immediately caught fire. The flames broke out among the Kentucky Baptists in Carroll County at the Ghent Baptist Church on the Ohio River. Great personalities emerged from the awakening, leaders such as Peter Cartwright and the circuit riders. Historian James Boles contends this movement actually gave birth to the so-called southeastern United States "Bible Belt."* American revivalistic evangelism, which continues to this day, received something of its impetus in this mighty movement. That is probably why the "Bible Belt" churches still call their annual evangelistic efforts "revivals," even if the name is now something of a misnomer.

Out of the frontier awakening, which actually formed a phase of America's Second Great Awakening, came a new motif of evangelism called the "camp meeting." The methodology spread all over the eastern United States and the revival radically transformed the entire frontier. The churches came alive as never before. In the pioneer communities, instead of gambling, cursing, and vice, a new spirituality, springing out of genuine Christian experience, characterized the early westward movement. God's sovereign hour had come to His people, and they humbled themselves before His power.

Then the evangelistic in-gathering started. From 1800 to 1804 the Baptists of Kentucky alone grew threefold; the Methodists fourfold. The Presbyterians doubled. That's revival! But we must never forget that the richness of the awakening emanated essentially from the sovereignty of God and God's people thus humbling themselves in response. Again let it be emphasized, He stands as the sole source of spiritual awakenings, and He grants these refreshing times in His sovereign grace and

---

*James Boles, *The Great Revival, 1787–1805,* (University of Kentucky Press, 1972).

time. And that surely becomes motive enough for us to humble ourselves. Such was the situation in Israel at the time of the great Exodus revival.

The Exodus Revival

No clearer insight into the basic revival principle of God's sovereignty and consequential human humility can be found than by looking into what was probably the greatest of all recorded Old Testament revivals: the extraordinary deliverance of Israel from Egypt in the second millennium B.C. Excluding the climactic "Christ event" itself, no act of God stands as more indicative of His sovereign grace than the Egyptian Exodus. It forms the focal point of Old Testament history and ultimately directs one's spiritual vision to God's redemption as finally and fully accomplished in Jesus Christ. Delving into the Exodus event and seeing the sovereignty of God revealed, we surely should "humble ourselves," as our theme text requires.

Moreover, an important principle regarding humility itself is set forth. Notice, we are to humble *ourselves*. God puts the responsibility to humble ourselves on us. He does not even urge us to pray for humility—we are to humble ourselves. But seeing God's absolute sovereignty unveiled, we do not find it difficult to prostrate ourselves at His feet in humble adoration.

The intriguing tale of Israel's redemption from Egypt is recorded in the early chapters of the Book of Exodus. The second book of the Bible stands as something to the Old Testament as the four Gospels do in the New; thus, it speaks of God's sovereign, reviving salvation. Its relevance to our lives today will become immediately apparent in this study of the Exodus awakening.

In Revival, God Reveals Himself as Sovereign

The principle of divine sovereignty becomes abundantly clear when one realizes the centrality of the *providence* of our Lord regarding His people. Exodus 1:7 states: "But the descendants of Israel were fruitful and increased greatly; they multiplied and grew exceedingly strong; so that the land was filled with them" (RSV).

Even though Israel lived as a subjugated people under the heavy hand of the Pharaohs, they prospered in the midst of their misery. God was certainly providentially at work among them.

The very fact that Israel found itself in Egypt speaks of God's sovereign acts; the story of Joseph and his family and its portrayal of Yahweh's providence make that clear. After a time, a new Pharaoh came to power, and soon they were reduced to misery and slavery. Of course, from a human perspective, it can be asked, "What is Israel doing in a place like Egypt? Why are they there? Why did God permit Joseph's brothers to treat him as they did? Genesis 46:3 answers that query: "God said to Jacob: 'I am God, the God of your father; do not be afraid to go down to Egypt; for I will there make of you a great nation'" (RSV). In simple terms, the sovereign God *chose* to put Israel in that strange land of bondage. He wanted to demonstrate what He alone could do through one man, Jacob, by raising him up, making him the progenitor of a great nation, and then through that chosen lineage redeem the whole world. That epitomizes sovereign providential grace.

Likewise, it can be asked today, why are we "the new Israel," where we are *spiritually*? So often we seem to suffer in a "strange land." Life can very easily slip out of joint. Bondage and fetters can quickly ensnare us. At times we all find ourselves in such a situation on our spiritual journey, and we quite naturally cry out, *why*? But could it be that God has put us, or at least permitted us, to be where we are so as to display what He alone in His sovereignty can do? Could He be designing our circumstances to make us a token of His sovereign providential grace? It just may be we are in "bondage" in our spiritual pilgrimage so He can most effectively perform and display His glory. We all long for God to reveal His glory, to do what He alone can do. Oh, to see the Lord's face, we sigh; to see God do something grand and unusual for ourselves, our homes, our churches, our country. Perhaps that can only happen in a "strange land."

The Rupert Revival

God did that sort of thing at Rupert, southwestern Vermont, in 1803. Before the significant movement of the Holy Spirit in

Rupert that year, the spiritual condition of the little community had degenerated and stagnated. God's blessings were abounding in other places; the so-called Second Great Awakening was underway. But Rupert remained untouched. Pastor John B. Preston lamented the fact that his church floundered on a sea of spiritual apathy. An Egyptian-type bondage had seemingly fettered God's activity among them. Deeply disturbed, a handful of the faithful realized no help would arise from any human source; God must move in sovereign grace. So the burdened believers banded together to pray once a week for revival. Their numbers were pitifully small—sometimes no more than two or three. Hardly any in the community felt real concern. Multitudes seemed content to enjoy the "fleshpots of Egypt." Nevertheless, the fervent prayers of the faithful few flowered. Quite suddenly, church attendance began to increase. The meetings grew increasingly solemn. Conviction began to fall. More people took to praying, and the number of prayer meetings multiplied to four. The pastor called for a day of public fasting and prayer. Something like the Old Testament "solemn assembly" emerged.

In November of 1803, "there came a sound from heaven" as the Spirit fell upon the church "like a rushing mighty wind" (Acts 2). It was as if another delightful Day of Pentecost had dawned. The effects were immediate. Scarcely a family could be found in the entire town in which there was not someone earnestly seeking salvation. New prayer meetings sprang up in every neighborhood. All sensed the profound solemnity of the presence of the Spirit. The day of God's glory had come. Preston wrote:

> It is impossible to describe the amazing change of appearance that took place within a few days. It was truly glorious to stand and see the salvation of God. How true, that when Zion travaileth she shall bring forth children. When Christians are enabled to open their eyes, and their hearts are enlarged in prayer, how soon the Lord cures their sore complaint and fills their souls with good![2]

The climax of the awakening in little Rupert came as eighty-four people were gloriously saved and added to the church. The revival subsequently spread to nearby communities. Six days of public fasting and prayer were held. With lives and churches transformed, the area finally witnessed one thousand new converts added to the kingdom. It does not take many to kindle revival fires, it simply takes sincerity, tenacity, and humility in the light of God's sovereignty and power to revive His people.

If we are to see similarly glorious things in our personal lives and in our needy churches and communities today, we must realize and accept the reality that the providence of God is at work, shaping circumstances, even difficult circumstances, so that He can display His reviving grace. Even if at the moment we suffer in an Egyptian time of cruel bondage, never forget: no Egypt, no Exodus. God surely has something glorious in mind, right in the face of our extremities. He does the most surprising things.

God's providence, however, proves very difficult to grasp at times. That is because our "Egypt" is usually a time of God's permitted *persecution*, perhaps even severe persecution. Israel surely felt that. The Bible says, "So they [the Egyptians] made the people of Israel serve with rigor, and made their lives bitter with hard service, in mortar and in brick, and in all kinds of work in the field; in all their work they made them serve with rigor" (Exodus 1:13–14, RSV). Why did God permit that to come on His people? It is somewhat understandable why God's providence put Israel in Egypt four hundred years; He was making of them a mighty nation. But why would God allow such extreme suffering in the meantime? We read that the Israelites literally "groaned" under life-sapping stress. And note, the Scriptures do not say they instituted organized prayer for deliverance. At that juncture their suffering was apparently such that all they seemingly could do was groan to God. They simply could not grasp what God was doing. If He is all powerful and *all-loving*, why did He permit all the suffering? That sort of situation invariably poses a real anomaly for the concept of God as a sovereign, yet loving Lord. Worst of all, we will probably *never* fully find a solution in this life. God does not always provide us answers for all our questions and quandaries. As Isaiah said, "Verily thou art a God that hidest thyself" (Isaiah 45:15, KJV). Is there then any hope?

The Israelites labored in anguish, waiting for someone to

come and cry to Pharaoh: "Let my people go." And they waited and waited! God apparently had turned a deaf ear their way. But the silence of God does not mean He is absent or oblivious to His people's cry. Appearances are not always realities. Little did Israel know God was preparing His servants right at that moment. God understands our stressful situations, and God knows all about the "bondage" under which we "groan." And God had heard their groanings (Exodus 3:23). The Scriptures state, "I am concerned about their suffering" (Exodus 3:7). If the sovereign God knows and is concerned, that is enough; we will humble ourselves and *rest in faith*, waiting for His redemption. And He will let us know all we need to know at the point where we are. Be assured of this: Regardless of the trial, redemption is at work. God is preparing His deliverance, right at this moment. As often said, our extremity is God's opportunity. God's grace often comes to us skillfully disguised as impossible situations. But there is an Exodus coming.

The Story of Luther

That beautiful Exodus principle exemplified itself one day many years ago as a bolt of lightning struck so close to a lonely traveler it knocked the young German miner's son to the ground. "Saint Anne," he cried out in terror, "I'll become a monk." As a good Roman Catholic, he kept his word and immediately moved into an Augustinian monastery.

It had been a sultry day in July of 1505, when the traveler trudged down the little lane on the outskirts of the old Saxon village of Satternheim. As he approached the village, a thunderstorm rolled in, and a clap of thunder and lightning prostrated him. His outcry was natural; St. Anne was the patron saint of miners. Martin Luther immediately joined the monastery at Wittenburg.

When Luther entered the monastery, little did he realize the trials he would face. To begin with, he moved into a personal crisis, a personal "Egypt" that drove him into deep despair. He became acutely conscious of his own sin. He would lie on the rough cot in his ice-cold cell in the bitter German winters, completely uncovered. Mortifying the flesh to atone for the sin of his soul became his aim. He even fasted to the point that he never recovered his complete health. One day as he was washing his hands he said to a fellow friar, "We wash and wash, but are never clean." The thunderstorm now raged in his sensitized soul. And then there was the church, the outward storm. The official church deeply grieved him at almost every point.

It all seemed very strange; the young monk prayed seven times a day. He confessed sins until he exhausted his confessor. Worshiping constantly, he attended mass day after day, earnestly seeking the salvation of his soul. Martin even took a pilgrimage to holy Rome, crawling up the Scala Santio on his knees. He exhausted the Roman system of indulgences. What next? One would have thought peace would ripple into his soul like a gentle stream, he was so sincere. But a raging wave of torrential terror all but overwhelmed him as his bondage deepened.

Why did the providence of God permit such suffering of the soul? What was God up to in Luther's life? Why the torture? He surely sought God. Why the "persecution"? Like Israel of old, God was about to display dramatically His sovereign grace and grant a great worldwide "Exodus."

At last, through studying the Bible, Luther discovered "the just shall live by faith," and he burst asunder the bonds of his "Egypt." From that point on Luther joyously heralded the glorious Good News, and soon the redemptive Reformation spread all over Europe. God's sovereignty providentially worked the "Exodus" of millions.

Never forget that God in His providence will *preserve* His redeemed in the midst of their providential persecutions. His providence not only redeems, it perseveres in the process. The sovereign God redemptively cares for His own. God saved Israel as a nation even when Pharaoh had determined their destruction. Here is another divine paradox: The Scriptures state, "But the more they were oppressed [God's people], the more they multiplied" (Exodus 1:12, RSV). No evil can defeat God's sovereign preservation of His people. Be assured that He can multiply His blessings even in the worst of trials.

The Bible tells us how God produced that puzzling paradox: "The midwives feared God, and did not as the king of Egypt commanded them, but let the male children live" (Exodus 1:17, RSV). Therefore, rest in faith, God in His sovereignty has a "midwife" to preserve us, even "multiply" us.

Can all of this be true? Can God's providence, permitted "persecution," and preservation be operative in the midst of our profound spiritual need? Yes, because in God's sovereign hand, He has a revival plan to see His name proclaimed throughout the earth. He even raised up Pharaoh, that wicked persecutor, in order to fulfill His plan of world redemption. Exodus 9:16 states, "In very deed for this cause have I raised thee up, for to shew in thee my power; and that my name may be declared throughout all the earth" (KJV). Paul reiterated the same verse to the Romans: "For the scripture saith unto Pharaoh, Even for this same purpose have I raised thee up, that I might shew my power in thee, and that my name might be declared throughout all the earth" (Romans 9:17, KJV). In some inscrutable sense, the "Pharaohs" we face today are there in God's ultimate wisdom and providence to renew and revive us and get the Gospel to the masses. Do not despair or fear them, God is working in history, because He is Lord. Revival will come in His planned sovereign time.

Therefore, as Peter urges, "Humble yourself . . . under the mighty hand of God, that he may exalt you *in due time*" (1 Peter 5:6, KJV). The reviving "due time" will come. God is never late. He was on time for the Israelites' Exodus; He will keep His schedule for ours. Thus, we are to "humble ourselves" and wait in faith on the sovereign God. Moreover, there is another significant spiritual awakening principle that springs out of the Exodus event: election.

God Sovereignly Elects in Revival

Election! There is a word that causes many to shudder. Yet, there was a time when it was a precious word to evangelicals. Whitefield, Edwards, Spurgeon, and other great revivalists cherished the idea. However, we have seemingly become so anthropologically centered today we seem to shun the concept. But election is a very stubborn biblical concept, constantly and consistently surfacing in the Scriptures. There is such a multitude of verses concerning divine election, Bible believers dare not ignore what the Scriptures state. The reluctance to face this issue may well have grown out of the perversions of the truth by the extremists. Still, we must never forget what Isaiah said about the sovereign Lord: "My counsel shall stand, and *I will do my pleasure*" (Isaiah 46:10, KJV). God will choose and elect to do as He pleases. He is Lord. He is not arbitrary, but He is Lord. He wants "both to will to do of *his* good pleasure" (Philippians 2:13, KJV). The Bible and all history demonstrates that fact, the Exodus event being a classic example. Looking at Israel's Exodus from Egypt in the context and light of God's sovereign election, four realities immediately stand out.

First, the *providence* of a reviving God rests in His sovereign grace. The story of the birth of Moses portrays dramatically the Lord's providence in election:

> Now a man from the house of Levi went and took to wife a daughter of Levi. The woman conceived and bore a son; and when she saw that he was a goodly child, she hid him three months. And when she could hide him no longer she took for him a basket made of bulrushes, and daubed it with bitumen and pitch; and she put the child in it and placed it among the reeds at the river's brink. . . . Now the daughter of Pharaoh came down to bathe at the river, and her maidens walked beside the river; she saw the basket among the reeds and sent her maid to fetch it. . . . Then his sister said to Pharaoh's daughter, "Shall I go and call you a nurse from the Hebrew women to nurse the child for you?" And Pharaoh's daughter said to her, "Go." So the girl went and called the child's mother. And Pharaoh's daughter said to her, "Take this child away, and nurse him for me, and I will give you your wages" (Exodus 2:1–3, 5, 7–9, RSV).

Why did God in His providence choose this particular family, and preserve this one child? *Because He did.* That is really the only answer we have. God simply did it in His own wisdom and acted in His own electing, sovereign grace. God has said through the prophet, "I have purposed, and I will do it" (Isaiah 46:11, RSV). That principle interweaves itself in all great redemptive revivals.

Secondly, look at the *persecution* permitted by a reviving God in election. "When Pharaoh heard of it, he sought to kill Moses. But Moses fled from Pharaoh, and stayed in the land of Midian" (Exodus 2:15, RSV). Why did God permit that? Again, *because He did.* The Scriptures never say it will be easy in the service of Christ. Quite the contrary! Actually, the closer we come to God's revival time, the more difficult it becomes.

Thirdly, the God of election will *preserve* His people in reviving power. "Now Moses kept the flock of Jethro, his father-in-law, the priest of Midian: and he led the flock to the backside of the desert" (Exodus 3:1, RSV). Why did God preserve Moses in that miserable desert? Why did not God cast Moses aside when he failed so miserably in Egypt. Why did He still have His hand on the man? *Because He did.* He elected to do so. But why the desert, of all places? The only rationale to that question centers in the fact that normally God's people must go through the "desert" before entering the "promised land." Although Moses was "exceeding fair" (Acts 7:20), "learned in all the wisdom of the Egyptians" (Acts 7:22), and "mighty in words and in deeds" (Acts 7:22), he needed to become "very meek" (Numbers 12:3). He needed to see God reveal himself in sovereign glory and thus humble himself. That took the "desert" to accomplish. For Moses it was even the "backside of the desert" (Exodus 3:1). It took God forty years to get Moses into a proper spiritual condition to be the deliverer of Israel. There were many rough edges that needed rounding off. Developing a true life of humility takes time, and often pain. The old self-life never gives up. But God must bring us to the end of ourselves before He can send reviving grace through us. Moses spent the first forty years of his life thinking he was somebody; the next forty years thinking he was nobody; and the last forty years realizing God in His reviving sovereignty can use anybody.

Finally, the sovereign *plan* of God in election always brings revival. God had devised a plan no one could even conceive of. He was about to fulfil that plan in the great Exodus awakening. And it all began by a little desert bush. What a scene emerged at the burning bush. God said, "Come now therefore, and I will send thee unto Pharaoh, that thou mayest bring forth my people the children of Israel out of Egypt" (Exodus 3:10, KJV). But again we ask, why is the sovereign God calling and sending this man? Moses himself apparently thought he had forfeited it all forty years earlier when he killed the Egyptian. From the human perspective he had. He questioned God saying, "Who am I, that I should go?" (Exodus 3:11, KJV). *But God chose him because He did.* Our Lord said, "I am come down to deliver

them" (Exodus 3:8, KJV), and *I choose you.* He reveals himself
as a reviving, redemptive Deliverer, and in His sovereignty He
elects whom He will. It is exactly as Paul wrote to the Thessalonians: "The one who calls you is faithful and he will do it"
(1 Thessalonians 5:24).

The call to deliver the Jews must have come like a thun-
derbolt to Moses. All the fears, frustrations, and feelings of
inadequacy whelmed up within him.* It boggled his mind to
the point that he contended with God. One of the amazing
things that surfaces in this fascinating encounter at the burning bush is that although God is sovereign, He still allows us
to "argue" with Him, even when He "comes down to deliver us."
Think of it: allowed to argue with the almighty, ultimate, electing, sovereign God! But realize, the Lord does not use only those
who are so spiritually mature that they never question His
purpose. His sovereignty and election even encompass those
who would question the Almighty! If He chose only perfectly
mature saints, He would choose very few. So He elected Moses,
a man who in many respects had been a constant failure up to
that point. Thus, Moses contends with God. The "argument"
must have gone something like this:

"Moses, go down to Egyptland and tell old Pharaoh, 'Let my
people go,' " saith the Lord.

"But God, who am I?" retorted Moses.

"Moses, go down," God repeated.

"But God, I failed at that before!"

"Moses!"

Just then, Moses thought he had the clincher in his case
against God's call: "But God, you know those Jews; you know
how they reacted when I tried to deliver them forty years ago.
They will surely say, 'Who sent you?' And God, I do not even
know your name."

At that moment God did something for Moses He had done
for no one before, not even Abraham, Isaac, and Jacob; God
revealed His own covenant name. What an event! God said,
"Moses, you tell them 'I AM' has sent you. I who was what I

---

*Moses seemingly had a genuine problem with feelings of inadequacy. Of
course, his entire life up to that point of the burning bush experience could
easily have precipitated those emotions. Apparently his faith was quite weak
at that time. Yet, God chose to use him. That is sovereign grace.

was, I who am what I am, I who will be what I will be: 'The same yesterday, and today, and forever.' You tell them *Yahweh, I AM*, has sent you."

Moses must have thought, "If that is who you are, if you are the Sovereign Eternal Lord, you must be adequate to enable me to fulfill your call." And although Moses still had some questions, if God is anything like His name, that is enough, and finally Moses decided, "I'll humble myself and go."

One principle to realize in this encounter revolves around the truth that the sovereign God, Yahweh, elects *all* His covenant people to go down and deliver the lost from their Egyptian bondage. Therefore, with Moses, we too had best humble ourselves *and go.*

God's absolute sovereignty in revival certainly does not nullify the responsibility of God's people to pray and seek revival. We are "to go" at God's bidding. We are not to fold our hands in superficial piety and passivity and just "wait on God." For example, early in 1799, the people of the small village of Farmington, Connecticut became deeply concerned for the spiritual situation of their church, community, and the cause of Christ generally. The pastor, Joseph Washburn, consulted with the leaders of the church and decided to call a meeting for prayer and consultation. The unanimous opinion of the people declared: "It was for us to pray, and for God, who is merciful and gracious, to dispose of events according to His own good pleasure." The truly repentant believers humbled themselves before the sovereign Lord and began to pray. Regular prayer meetings were held so that, as they said, "God would not pass us by." God did not pass them by. In His sovereign purpose, He uses humble prayer. Revival came to Farmington, and sixty-one people found Christ and were brought into the little church. Sovereign grace always accomplishes redemption and salvation.

God Is Sovereignly Redemptive in Revival

The ultimate goal of any spiritual awakening centers in the sovereign God redeeming people. This is axiomatic. The Exodus event set forth this principle as a pattern for all time. The scene is most dramatic: There are the Israelites at the Red Sea; the waters are before them, the Egyptians behind them. What a plight! But hear God's Word: "Moses said unto the people, Fear ye not, stand still, and see the salvation of the LORD, which he will shew to you today: for the Egyptians whom ye have seen today, ye shall see them again no more for ever. The LORD shall fight for you, and ye shall hold your peace" (Exodus 14:13–14, KJV). That which looked like a wall was really a door, and a people who had been held long in bondage were born free.

What a wonderful promise: "The LORD shall fight for you." When God redeems a people, He becomes their warrior. As the Scriptures state, "The battle is the LORD's" (1 Samuel 17:47, KJV). That stands as true today as in Moses' time. Therefore, we believers will be very wise to humble ourselves and "hold our peace." As one commentator put it, "Though all the powers of evil array themselves against us, whatever God has called us to do will issue precisely as He has appointed."[3] God always reveals himself as sovereign *Redeemer*.

The consequences of God's providence in redemption are thrilling. Hear Moses and Israel sing: "I will sing to the LORD, for he has triumphed gloriously" (Exodus 15:1, RSV). The "joy of the LORD" (Nehemiah 8:10, RSV) became their strength. This principle explains why awakened Christians have always been a singing people. In writing to the church in Ephesus, Paul stated we are to be "filled with the Spirit, addressing one another in psalms and hymns and spiritual songs, singing and making melody to the Lord with all your heart" (Ephesians 5:18–19, RSV). Spurgeon, in his eloquent style, said, "A genuine revival without joy in the Lord is as impossible as spring without flowers, or day dawn without light . . . let us abound in holy joy and make it our constant delight to joy in God."[4]

But what about today? It has been over 3000 years since the exciting Exodus. Not only that, well over a century has passed since the great Prayer Revival of 1858, which became the last nation-sweeping revival America and Britain experienced, although some areas were blessed in the Welsh Revival of 1904.* The question is, can we see the providence of a sovereign, redeeming God at work today precipitating the next great awak-

---

*A profound stirring of the spirit, commonly called the Welsh Revival, swept across many lands in 1904. Yet, it did not possess the profundity of the Prayer Revival.

ening? That same basic query was put to revivalist Charles G. Finney in the 1830s, a few short years before the Prayer Revival. He had his answer for his day—perhaps for ours also.

Can We Expect Revival Today?

Finney finds the prophet Habakkuk praying the proper prayer when revival is fermenting: "O LORD, revive thy work in the midst of the years, in the midst of the years make known; in wrath remember mercy" (Habakkuk 3:2, KJV). The prophet anticipated anguish; Judah's defeat and captivity hovered close at hand. Difficulties abounded throughout the land. God was their only hope. So he prayed, "O Lord, revive thy work."

Finney contends this sort of situation can prepare the stage for the drama of an awakening. When society and the church degenerates, just when it seems there could never be a move of God, that can be the divine moment.

Further, Finney argues that an awakening becomes essential when brotherly love wanes. He states, "When there are dissensions, and jealousies, and evil speakings . . . then there is a great need of revival."[5] This clearly speaks to much of our contemporary church life. I know of a congregation that actually split and divided into two churches over which side of the building to place the piano. It would be humorous if it were not so sad. Yet, a degenerate society and church often becomes a positive sign for a forthcoming awakening.

Finney goes on to contend that when worldliness grips the people of God, a revival is desperately needed. Yet, that situation can be a harbinger of a coming renewal. In times past, Christians have been sensitive about worldly plans and ways, ambitions, pleasures, and carnal values. Now, it seems we have not only let down the barriers, we have become blasé about it.

Open sin in the congregation also points to the need of new life, Finney tells us. Years ago church discipline—even if not well-handled at times—dealt with these issues. Now, church members can commit adultery, deal deceitfully in business, curse, and tell off-color stories with impunity.

Finally, when the lost live in unconcern, even when they hear the Gospel, an awakening is sorely needed. But it is right in the midst of such depressing circumstances that God often steps in and revives His work. Discerning believers know that only the presence of the sovereign God in quickening power makes the Good News alive.

If these are the conditions preceding a revival, as Finney argues, when will the awakening itself actually come? It is obvious that we have this sort of situation today. What do we yet lack?

Finney replies by declaring that a revival is just about to break when the "wickedness of the wicked grieves and humbles and distresses Christians."[6] That Victorian expression simply means, when we finally get sick and tired of the moral corruption, violence, and spiritual unconcern that abounds all around, God will do something for His distressed people. Surely we are aware that ethical and moral corruption has obliterated every civilization in history, the classic case being Rome. And remember, those who forget history are doomed to relive it. Most serious of all, people stand under the judgment of God.

Of course, it should be clear that it is not the reality and presence of evil that precipitates awakenings. When wickedness prevails, one of two things normally happens to the church. Either the church grieves and begins to agonize humbly before God, thus precipitating healing, or the church makes peace with the situation and grows increasingly corrupt and compromising, hence losing its testimony and power. But when the church compromises, judgment comes. Christians should, therefore, *grieve* over sinful situations. If revival is to come, the only hope rests in believers becoming deeply disturbed, distressed, and humbled. Finney put it like this: "If Christians are made to feel that they have no hope but in God, and if they have sufficient feeling left to care for the honor of God, and the salvation of the souls of the impenitent, there will certainly be a revival."[7] Evil may abound, but if God's people prevail in prayer, the Lord will raise up a standard. Finney said, "I have known instances where a revival has broken in upon the ranks of the enemy, almost as suddenly as a clap of thunder, and scattered them—taking the very ringleaders as trophies, and breaking up their party in an instant."[8]

This leads to another vital principle; namely, an awakening is ready to burst on the dismal scene when Christians have a deep, profound Spirit of prayer for an awakening. Prayer has been emphasized often, but notice, what is called for is a Spirit of prayer for revival *specifically*. We pray for the sick, the missionaries, those in trouble, give thanks for the nice day, etc.— and rightly so. But, where is the Spirit of prayer for an awakening? Where are the agonizers for a visitation of God? Where are the broken hearts for the lost? Paul cried, "My little children, with whom I am again in travail" (Galatians 4:19). That exemplifies the attitude that brings down heaven and all its blessings. Leonard Ravenhill put his finger on it in his book *Sodom Had No Bible* when he said, "The church is dying on its feet because it is not living on its knees."

If only a handful of praying people could be found; for the number of the burdened believers is irrelevant to the degree of blessing. Finney tells of one dedicated woman in a church who became heart-burdened and anxious for the unconverted. She devoted herself to prayer for their salvation. Her distress and anxiety heightened until she pleaded with her pastor to call a special meeting to reach the lost. The minister put her off; he felt no such concern. She persisted—so did he. Finally, she came to him and said, "If you do not appoint a meeting I shall die, for there is certainly going to be a revival." He relented and the next Sunday invited all who might be concerned for their salvation to a special meeting to seek God. He did not know of one concerned person. But to his amazement, an unbelievable number responded. How did the dear woman know? The secret of the Lord was with her. A broken heart and an agonizing prayer burden bring spiritual awakenings.

Where are we today? Does the Spirit of prayer prevail? If not, then we should pray for the Holy Spirit of prayer to fall. Most of us probably need to begin by praying for the power of the Spirit to enable us to pray. The Spirit of prayer cannot be conjured up soley by human energy. God's Spirit must come and lay the prayer burden on our very souls. It is the *Holy Spirit* of prayer we need, not simply a human spirit of prayer. He is the one who "intercedes for the saints according to the will of God" (Romans 8:27, RSV).

Finney further says that revival comes when ministers of the Gospel become burdened for revival. When this happens, the awakening may soon break. Pastors and leaders are constantly pulled in a thousand different directions. It is often hard for them to keep focused on the essentials! To keep priorities straight constitutes no easy task. Yet God has placed ministers in key leadership roles. Therefore, God's people tend to become what their leaders are. They adopt their leaders' views, system of values, styles of ministry, and sense of needs. A burdened pastor promotes a burdened congregation. A renewal-oriented leader develops a revival-oriented people. Ministers should ask themselves, "What truly matters in my ministry?"

Finney goes on to remark that awakening enters on the stage of sacrifice. When Christians are found willing to make the necessary sacrifices, the revival may surely be on the way. Real awakening will cost highly in time and energy. It can cost reputation and material gain. Some people will be very resistant to the movement. Conflict is inevitable. Therefore, one must be willing to forfeit "respect" among the world's crowd. At times the "world's crowd" is actually found in the church. There is a price to pay, and God's true people must pay it.

Not only that, Finney points out we must permit God to promote the awakening in any way and by whatever instruments *He chooses.* Even that can be a sacrifice, for we often seem willing to have a revival, provided we can run it our way, as we see fit. But God will not be hamstrung. His ways may be quite different from ours. He will often take the most unlikely people and thereby glorify himself. It was surely true in Corinth. Paul reminded that church:

> For consider your call, brethren; not many of you were wise according to worldly standards, not many were powerful, not many were of noble birth; but God chose what is foolish in the world to shame the wise, God chose what is weak in the world to shame the strong, God chose what is low and despised in the world, even things that are not, to bring to nothing things that are, so that no human being might boast in the presence of God (1 Corinthians 1:26–29, RSV).

The Holy Spirit laid His hands on a simple, uneducated shoe salesman and molded him into the great D. L. Moody; lifted up a drunken baseball player off a Chicago street and made him evangelist Billy Sunday; touched a lanky North Carolina farm boy and fashioned a Billy Graham who has preached the Gospel to more people face-to-face than anyone in the history of Christianity.

Means as well as people may be far different from our expectations. Often the Baptists think it *must* be a Baptist revival, and the Methodists a Methodist awakening, and the Pentecostals a Pentecostal one. Yet God will choose whom and what He pleases. He stands sovereign in all awakenings. God's way may well shock us all, especially the religious establishment. Still, we must let God control the awakening. His wisdom is best and His means will bring the greatest glory to himself. We must be honestly humble and let the sovereign God be God.

Finally, we can expect a revival, as Finney expressed it, when God's providence indicates an awakening is at hand. At times the signs stand out in bold relief; other times they shroud themselves in obscurity. Yet, revival harbingers begin to be discerned by spiritually sensitive believers. When all the principles discussed above are at work, openly or quietly, a revival is surely in the wings, waiting for God's cue to come center stage. Moreover, God longs to give us an awakening. That should give great encouragement. Finney sums it up by stating:

> Strictly, I should say that when the foregoing things occur, a revival, to the same extent, already exists. In truth a revival should be expected whenever it is needed. Therefore, whenever the church needs reviving they ought and may expect to be revived, and to see sinners converted to Christ. When those things are seen which are named under the foregoing heads, let Christians and ministers be encouraged and know that a good work is already begun.[9]

Finney is surely correct. But are there any really positive signs today?

When God first opened my heart to the reality and challenge of spiritual awakening during student days in seminary, I was tremendously enthused to realize that God did such marvelous things in revival. But when speaking of revival or preaching on it, most hearers had a rather indifferent attitude. A few came alive to the theme, but only a few. I began to feel like John the Baptist: "The voice of one crying in the wilderness." But today, how different it is! Thank God for the new concern, interest, and prayer for a fresh spiritual awakening that abounds everywhere. Polster George Gallup tells us that in 1970, at the height of the youth protest movement, only 14% of the American people saw religion as gaining influence in the country, while 75% felt it was loosing ground. Today over 44% believe religion is gaining influence while only 42% see it losing. Things are on the upbeat. Prayer for a spiritual awakening is becoming a major theme. Prayer groups are being raised up across the world. Jonathan Edwards' old "Concert of Prayer" for spiritual awakening is being called for once more and many are responding. Eyes are trained on those parts of our world where revival fires burn such as South Korea, East Africa, Brazil, and Eastern Europe. People are beginning to long for a deep and profound renewing. Surely the gracious providence of the sovereign God has brought us to this place. The new sense of burden has given birth to a firm conviction among many that once again God is about to rend the heavens and mightily revive His work. When the awakening comes, the Methodists, Presbyterians, Pentecostals, Baptists, Independents, Roman Catholics, etc., will all share in the glory of God's sovereign awakening power. He is Lord of all. Many believe a new Exodus is just about to begin, just as it did for Israel under Moses. When they cried to God, He heard from heaven.

Israel's Cry for Revival

Hear Israel pleading with God:

And it came to pass in process of time, that the king of Egypt died: and the children of Israel sighed by reason of the bondage, and they cried, and their cry came up unto God by reason of the bondage. And God heard their groaning, and God remembered His covenant with Abraham, with Isaac, and with Jacob (Exodus 2:23–24, KJV).

It seems it always takes persecution of some sort to drive believers to humble themselves. But if it takes persecution to drive God's people to their knees, then may God permit it. And surely there is enough of it around for Israel in the past and for us in the present hour to humble ourselves before God. But whenever a people have truly humbled themselves and cried out to the Lord, as was true of Israel just before the Exodus,

"God heard . . . and remembered" (Exodus 2:24). Never forget
that the preservation of God in redemption can be relied upon.
He told the heartbroken Israelites, "I have surely seen the affliction of my people which are in Egypt, and have heard their
cry by reason of their taskmasters; for I know their sorrows"
(Exodus 3:7, KJV). He knows. He cares. He revives.

The Revival Plan

Now, when all these principles come together under God's
sovereign purpose, His redemption *plan* bursts forth. Hear His
promise: "I am come down to deliver them out of the hand of
the Egyptians, and to bring them up out of that land unto a
good land and a large, unto a land flowing with milk and honey"
(Exodus 3:8, KJV). Redeem them, God did. The prophets, the
psalmist, all Israel never tired telling of our Lord's great Exodus redemption. O for the day when God will come down to
deliver us from our contemporary bondage. We desperately
need to see His Exodus power displayed once more. We will see
it if we humble ourselves under His sovereignty and cry out in
intense intercession as Israel in Egypt has taught us.

There is an event in the life of Sir Winston Churchill that
illustrates and can teach us how we should pray. At the end of
World War II, Britain's prime minister retired. As an old man,
Churchill was invited to address the students at his alma ma-
ter, Harrow School, an exclusive boys' school in the northern
suburbs of London. As the veteran politician rose to the podium,
the boys probably wondered how it was that after so many early
failures in life he had become such a successful leader in his
later years. (Churchill's younger life was actually filled with
failure after failure.) When the war broke out he promised the
British people nothing but "blood, sweat, tears, and toil" during
the terrible years; yet, he surely did give them their "finest
hour." His record as a leader became legendary in his time.
How to account for that marvelous success at the end of his life
must have been a mystery to the lads. But the great orator did
not leave them in doubt. In his speech he reared back, as he
was prone to do, looked the lads straight in the eyes and said,
"Young men, *never give in! Never give in! Never! Never!*

NEVER! NEVER! In anything great or small, large or petty—*never give in!*"

Our Lord said, "The kingdom of heaven suffereth violence, and the violent take it by force" (Matthew 11:12, KJV). We must "violently" bombard heaven with our prayers for revival and never give in. *Never! Never! NEVER! NEVER!* Then the sovereign God will hear, rend the sky and pour out a deluge of revival blessing. Therefore, we must humble ourselves and let God be God. The revival will come out of His sovereign will and in His sovereign time and will display His sovereign grace. *PRAY!*

At Last, a Leader Who Leads

In a Spiritual Awakening God Reveals Himself as

HOPE

Therefore, "Seek His Face."
2 CHRONICLES 28–32

Introduction

The cohesive cultural fabric that had always held Jewish society together was coming apart at the seams. King Ahaz, one of Judah's most wicked tyrants, had all but devastated the nation and dashed to the ground the people's hope for better days. Despair, dismay, and depression descended like a blanket of smog on the entire populace. The oppressive atmosphere was heavy with hopelessness. It boded that the year 736 B.C. could be the Southern Kingdom's last.

What gave birth to such a serious social situation? The answer is simple: sin. The social problem was a spiritual problem—it always is. King Ahaz's rebellion against God had virtually led the entire nation astray and into the jaws of judgment. The scenario the Scriptures sketch of the Jews during Ahaz's reign is painted with broad brush strokes of doom and devastation. How could anything save such a people? Hope had dissipated.

When Society Leaves God

The Bible says about foolish King Ahaz: "He walked in the ways of the kings of Israel" (2 Chronicles 28:2). Ahaz made the tragic decision of building his value system on the level of this world's understanding of truth, meaning, and reality. And the Jews of Judah soon followed suit. They should have known better; God had warned them repeatedly through the prophets. But they were a new generation and failed to realize that "all that is in the world, the lust of the flesh, and the lust of the eyes, and the pride of life, is not of the Father, but is of the world. And the world passeth away, and the lust thereof" (1

John 2:16–17, KJV). They had willfully rejected the prophets' cry and forgotten God's gracious dealings with them in the past. Thus, they were swept away into a maelstrom of materialism, the temporal, the thrilling, the fleshly, the ego satisfying: *the sinful*. What a tragedy! What a striking portrait it paints of our present society.

To draw an analogy with contemporary society and its system of values is, of course, unnecessary. A cursory glance at today's covetous, carnal lifestyle, with its inordinate sensual quest for the "good life," makes Israel sound very much up-to-date. Many in the whole western world will seemingly do almost anything to build up their materialistic bank account and live in the "fast lane." They will compromise convictions, cut moral corners, use other people as a ladder, even resort to violence. The worship of the golden calf of greed and power fascinates the fashionable. And that is not to mention the subsequent escape into drugs, alcohol, sex, utter selfishness, and even suicide.

These lifestyles often force people into crime and inhuman violence. The very day these lines were being penned, the local newspaper headlines read:

"Edmond Woman Slain . . ."
"Two More Arrested in Hijacking"
"Judge Lets Vigilante Go Free"
"Slaying Suspects' Arraignment on Hold"
"Porn Laws Challenged by Suspect"
"Man Pleads Guilty to Murder"
"Man Guilty in Youth's Death"
And on and on. . . .

Moreover, this is just an average Wednesday's reporting in a city not of exceptionally large population. There is a murder approximately every twenty minutes in the United States. A large city newspaper had a headline that read "Murder Runs Wild."

Along with the drug problem, world hunger, the rage of the disenfranchised, and the ungodly grasp for power, one day some wild world leader will surely "push the button." Regardless of the dramatic changes in Eastern Europe, there are still many buttons of various sorts to push. Then, utter despair! Our day, as in Ahaz's time, is also a time of depressing hopelessness.

What shall we do? Is there really any hope at all?

A glad and happy affirmative can be given to this foundational question. *There is hope!* And the reason is so simple, yet so profound; hopelessness and despair grow out of disregard for God. When a person or a people part from God, despair soon sets in. But the God of hope can alter the entire dismal dynamic, in our day as well as in Ahaz's. Society can be turned Godward and a new day dawn. Revival and renewal really are possible. Take heart, God always reveals himself as "hope" in revival. Therefore, the wise "seek His face," as our theme text urges.

Israel's Degeneration

It seems society must often sink to the depths of moral degeneration before it is shocked into consciousness concerning the dire need of renewal and thus begin to lift up its eyes and seek God. A hard look at that downward spiraling spiritual syndrome as it occurred in Ahaz's reign will provide us with much instruction. The Bible catalogues the characteristics of his ungodly reign.

The ruinous rule of Ahaz became *a time of gross idolatry*: "He even made molten images for the Baals" (2 Chronicles 28:2, RSV). The term "Baal" means "Lord." The Israelites made the spiritual blunder of thinking Baal was a living lord with might and majesty. The Jews viewed Baal as the god of productivity, the lord of abundance. They actually believed he could produce good crops, fruits, animals, and even people. When droughts and famine ravaged the land, the worshipers went to unbelievable lengths to curry Baal's favor. They utterly failed to see that the true and living God understands people in their needs and can abundantly help them. Tragically, Israel, who had the revelation of the true God, looked to the wrong source to supply their legitimate needs; they turned to Baal where no need could ever really be met.

Not only that, "he (Ahaz) burnt incense in the valley of the son of Hinnom" (2 Chronicles 28:3, KJV). This brand of idolatrous worship centered in the adoration of the god Molech. This hideous heathen idol was set up in the Valley of Hinnom, directly south of Jerusalem. Molech would be heated up to incandescence; then, the sick, perverted worshipers would throw their own precious children into his flaming arms. What a wicked, vicious way to appease a false god. Ahaz himself, "burned his sons as an offering, according to the abominable practices of the nations" (2 Chronicles 28:3, RSV). Later the Valley of Hinnom became the city garbage dump, and the fires and stench constantly rose in the nostrils of the people. It presented an odious, obnoxious scene. This is the very spot Jesus used to describe hell: "gehenna," the Valley of Hinnom. And it became a "hell" for Israel.

One can understand and deeply empathize with a people wrought with despair during a time of severe need. But Ahaz and his people were so far from God they turned to a dry fountain hoping to find a cup of cool water. All they got was dust. The results: "Ahaz, king of Israel, made Judah naked" (2 Chronicles 28:19, KJV). The word "naked" means to cast aside all restraints. They ran wild. They split their moral seams. Everything came apart. They utterly and completely forgot God's promise: "If my people who are called by my name humble themselves, and pray and seek my face, and turn from their wicked ways, then I will hear from heaven, and will forgive their sin and *heal their land*" (2 Chronicles 7:14). As a result, they suffered severe consequences. Weakness and erosion ate away at every area of national life.

Moreover, as could be expected, military weakness inevitably followed. That was important to the Jews, for Israel viewed military weakness as tantamount to spiritual weakness. Such was the mind-set of the eighth century B.C. The final outcome arrived: "Therefore the LORD his God gave him [Ahaz] into the hand of the king of Syria, who defeated him and took captive a great number of his people and brought them to Damascus" (2 Chronicles 28:5, RSV). Two hundred thousand women and children were carried into captivity (2 Chronicles 28:8). Even Pekah, the ruler of the Northern Kingdom of Israel, slaughtered one hundred twenty thousand fellow Jews of the Southern Kingdom in a devastating battle. The moral degeneration of the times went so far as to pit brother against brother.

Then, diplomatic frustration rumbled in like an avalanche. The complete court swirled in turmoil. Ahaz did not know where to turn. The Edomites and Philistines were constantly raiding Judah, and Ahaz was so diplomatically and militarily weak he could not offset the onslaught. So he "sent to the king of Assyria for help" (2 Chronicles 28:16). He had erroneously turned to Baal for productivity; now he turned to Assyria for military protection when he knew God had said, "The battle is the LORD's" (2 Chronicles 20:15). Poor, benighted Ahaz did not realize what Isaiah meant when the prophet said there is no help "in the chariots of Egypt" (Isaiah 31:1). He even went so far as to take the sacred artifacts of the house of the Lord and give them to the Assyrian king, Tilgath-pilneser. Did all that conniving avail anything? Did Ahaz get his costly help? Hardly! The Bible says, "Tilgath-pilneser king of Assyria came against him, and afflicted him instead of strengthening him" (2 Chronicles 28:20, RSV). One would have thought that such defeat would shock Ahaz and Judah into facing reality. But, inconceivable as it seems, "In the time of his distress he became yet more faithless to the LORD" (2 Chronicles 28:22, RSV). He slammed shut the doors of the house of the Lord (v. 24) and erected idols on every street corner. How low can a leader and a people sink?

It is always that way, however, when the Lord's restraints are thrown off. Even "friends" turn into enemies. We live in a morally ordered universe; cast godliness aside and this world will turn to devour us. It does little good to cry, "Where is God?" in the midst of problems and perplexities, if we as a people have departed from God. So the people of Judah stumbled along and tried to muddle through their problems in a spirit of despair and hopelessness: "The LORD brought Judah low" (2 Chronicles 28:19, KJV). Degradation! Depression! Desperation! Hopelessness!

The situation in Judah under Ahaz sounds much like the deplorable conditions in eighteenth-century England just before the Great Awakening. Religiously, the country had lost most of its spiritual moorings. The Anti-Puritan legislation passed between 1661 and 1665 seriously eroded the entire spiritual life of England. At the restoration of Charles II, the king promised a general amnesty for the faithful, but he soon recanted. The newly elected Parliament proved to be "hot royalists and hot Churchmen"; spiritual Christianity and evangelical thought were in serious jeopardy. Under Charles, Parliament passed four devastating edicts:

1. *The Corporation Act (1661):* it eliminated Puritan political influence.
2. *The Act of Uniformity (1662):* the Prayer Book was revised, all clergymen had to swear by it. Two thousand evangelical clergymen were ejected from the Church of England, one-fifth of all their ministers.
3. *The Convention Act (1664):* this forbade evangelicals to meet in homes with more than five people. The result if caught three times: fines and imprisonment.
4. *The Five-Mile Act (1665):* non-conformists could not build a church within five miles of any town; the fine being 40 pounds and six months in jail.

Later came the *Expulsion of Non-Jurors* (1689–1690). This act of legislation seriously depressed the evangelical cause even further. Some relief came under William III, but then high churchmen, forced through the "Oath of Allegiance," and another 400 evangelical ministers left the Church of England. Along with the "Suppression of Convocation," the "Conformity Act of 1711," and the "Schism Act of 1714," the evangelical cause hovered on the verge of collapse. Furthermore, the remaining Anglican clergy were so worldly that many of them were utter profligates. Deism and rationalism reigned in the minds of the people. The whole religious scene had become dismal indeed.

Spiritually and morally, the entire country foundered. A popular slogan was "Get drunk for a penny, dead drunk for two pence." The clergy were known as the "blind guides," as one historian put it:

> It was the time when, as Johnson cynically observed, "The Apostles were tried regularly once a week on charge of committing forgery" . . . this . . . spread until the spiritual life became numbed and dead. "The English clergy of the day," says one observer, "are the most remiss of their labours in private, and the least severe in their lives." The system of "pluralities" still further reduced their status. Many of the clergy, while enjoying their revenues, never resided or even saw their benefices. Green quotes a Welsh bishop who boasted that he had never seen his diocese but once, and that he habitually resided at the [beautiful] lakes of . . . [England].[1]

The following quotation from *Green's Short History of the*

English People will suffice to sum up the situation:

> Of the prominent statesmen of the time the greater part
> were unbelievers in any form of Christianity, and were dis-
> tinguished for the grossness and immorality of their lives.
> Drunkenness and foul talk were thought no discredit to
> Walpole. A later Prime Minister, the Duke of Grafton, was
> in the habit of appearing with his mistress at the play. Pu-
> rity and fidelity to the marriage vow were sneered out of
> fashion, and Lord Chesterfield in his letters to his son, in-
> structs him in the art of seduction as part of a polite edu-
> cation.[2]

Moral despair reigned.

Is there any hope when gloom and despair prevail and such deplorable conditions permeate a people? Could God work among such conditions? Notice, in Israel's case under Ahaz, the Bible declares it was *the Lord* who brought Judah low.* If so, there is hope. God was still at work for Israel—and for His people in any century, even if He works in judgment and "brings them low." The dark cloud of judgment always has the silver lining of hope, for God is behind it. And He always reveals himself as a God of hope, a God of reviving hope, even when multitudes depart from Him. Judgment can actually be the harbinger of revival. He awakened the English in the depressing eighteenth century. One day the giants John Wesley and George Whitefield burst on the scene and a great revival soon followed. The church and society were revolutionized. We live in the legacy of that awakening to this day. Remember, He certainly revived Israel even after Ahaz had made virtual havoc of the land. What God did in the past, He can do again for us. Therefore, those in need of revival are to see God as hope and "seek His face."

The Revival Begins

First, Ahaz died. God's providence removed the first real obstacle. Under Ahaz's reign, the people suffered seriously for

---

*This does not imply God was responsible for the conditions or caused the sin. He simply let sin do its destructive work. He was there all the time using those circumstances to turn people's eyes on himself.

their spiritual infidelity. Yet it must be realized that leaders are important, and if God cannot renew them, He may well remove them one way or another. Sin in leaders is serious—to themselves personally and to those whom they lead. That may sound harsh to shallow, sentimental ears, but God's judgment is sure. The wages of sin is still death (Romans 3:23). In our day of superficial "positive thinking," we must not forget that God has called us to be a "holy people," called apart for Him.

Then, we read, "Hezekiah his son reigned in his stead" (2 Chronicles 28:27, KJV). That tremendous turn of events brought hope for a real revival. With the ascent of Hezekiah to the throne, God began preparing His people for a new spiritual awakening just waiting to sweep the land. As seen earlier, James Burns in *Revivals: Their Laws and Leaders* states that one of the prime principles of a spiritual awakening is "the emergence of the prophet." God so often raises up one who will fearlessly lift high His standard and become His spokesman for renewal. Could this young king be that emerging prophet?

Of course, it was not that there were no God-called prophets in the land during the time of Israel's despair. The great Isaiah powerfully prophesied during those bleak days. He told Judah plainly and fearlessly:

The ox knows its owner,
    and the ass its master's crib;
but Israel does not know,
    my people does not understand.
Ah, sinful nation,
    a people laden with iniquity,
offspring of evildoers,
    sons who deal corruptly!
They have forsaken the LORD,
    they have despised the Holy One of Israel,
    they are utterly estranged.

Why will you still be smitten,
    that you continue to rebel?
The whole head is sick,
    and the whole heart faint.
From the sole of the foot even to the head,
    there is no soundness in it,
but bruises and sores
    and bleeding wounds;

they are not pressed out, or bound up,
or softened with oil.

Your country lies desolate,
your cities are burned with fire;
in your very presence
aliens devour your land;
it is desolate, as overthrown by aliens.
(Isaiah 1:3–7, RSV)

That scene sounds very negative. But some negatives are real. Yet, even in the midst of judgment, God always stands ready to show mercy to those who realize their desperate situation, repent of their dastardly sin, and return to the Savior. He is a God of hope in revival. There is forgiveness with the Lord. So we should seek Him with all our hearts. Remember, Isaiah went on to say:

Come now, let us reason together,
says the LORD:
though your sins are like scarlet,
they shall be as white as snow;
though they are red like crimson,
they shall become like wool.
If you are willing and obedient,
you shall eat the good of the land.
(Isaiah 1:18–19, RSV)

But would Judah hear?

Moreover, the prophet Hosea was also pleading in the Spirit's power at that time. After the amazing illustration of God's love that Hosea exemplified in his own family life, he cried out to wayward, adulterous Judah as they went whoring after their idols, "Return unto the LORD thy God; for thou hast fallen by thine iniquity" (Hosea 14:1, KJV). Micah, another contemporary prophet, preached, "He has showed you, O man, what is good; and what does the LORD require of you but to do justice, and to love kindness, and to walk humbly with your God?" (Micah 6:8, RSV). Surely, some must have heard the prophets' cry. Some must have responded. It had to be true that some were moved by God's forgiving love. The remnant had to be there. Isaiah tells us a small remnant remained that still loved the Lord (Isaiah 1:9). God never fails to leave himself a witness.

It is through that godly remnant, no matter how small, that God can work and bring hope for revival. The remnant can be His "salt of the earth" to save and preserve a decaying people.

The Emergence of the Prophet

The emerging man amidst this godly remnant whom God chose to effect the actual awakening at this juncture of Judah's history was not a prophet in the strictest sense; rather, it proved to be the young King Hezekiah. What an unusual man. Yet, this was not the only time in spiritual awakenings that God used royalty to bring a great revival to the land.

The year was 1727 in Saxony. On the lordly estate called Herrnhut (the "Lord's watch") young Count Ludwig von Zinzendorf earnestly sought revival. His dedication was exemplary. He pleaded for the Lord's blessings for decades. Then suddenly on Wednesday, August 13, 1727, God honored that diligent seeking. The full bloom of revival blessings burst forth. During a communion service, God opened the heavens on Herrnhut and a great awakening occurred.

It had all begun some years earlier when the young Count entered the University of Halle in Germany. Sitting at the feet of Professor August Francke, one of the leading academics of Halle, Zinzendorf began his studies. Francke, along with his scholarship, was a deeply devoted man of God. He saw himself as a "pietist," having imbibed deeply of the spirit of the great pietist pastor of Berlin, Philipp Jakob Spener.

In those dynamic days, the University of Halle shone as the pietistic north star of the Lutheran Church, guiding thousands to a devout spiritual harbor. Contrary to what some would have us believe, the mature pietists were not other-worldly dreamers. They simply believed in a vital, daily experience of Jesus Christ based on the Bible.

Young Count Zinzendorf proudly claimed pastor Spener as his godfather, and while at Halle took his noon meals in Professor Francke's home. Zinzendorf drank deeply of the pietistic "elixir." The spiritual fervor created a deep thirst for God's very best. Soon, his heart hungered for revival.

After completing his education, Count Zinzendorf returned to Herrnhut. About that time, Moravian Brethren began seeking asylum at Zinzendorf's estate. They were the old Hussites from Moravia—centered in Prague—where they had been under serious persecution for their evangelical faith. A sizeable community of devout Christians developed at Herrnhut.

Led by Zinzendorf, the Brethren began praying for revival. The Lord poured the Spirit of prayer on their burdened hearts, and they lingered long before God crying for an awakening. On occasion they would pray all night. Their concern for a spiritual revival deepened as the months went by. Then one beautiful Lord's day, while in worship, God drew out his sword and ripped open the heavens. The Moravian Revival commenced. What a day it was; and its spiritual ramifications spread far and wide. We have seen the Moravian impact on world missions and on John Wesley. But who would have thought that a sophisticated man of nobility could have been so used in a spiritual awakening? Yet, there is the beautiful scriptural precedent to God's use of young Count Zinzendorf: young King Hezekiah.

What did Hezekiah do to seek a spiritual awakening in his day? If we learn Hezekiah's secret, perhaps we can seek the face of this God of hope as he did.

The Commencement of Israel's Reform

Bible scholars point out that the Hezekiah revival stands as one of the most sudden, unexpected movements recorded in Scripture. The new king ascended the throne and in two months the entire countryside glowed with revival glory. How did it all happen so soon?

It will help first of all to see what sort of man Hezekiah actually was. He certainly did not participate in the sins of his wicked father Ahaz—nor in their judgment. Of course, Hezekiah certainly was not perfect, he shared in the fallen race. But he adamantly refused to walk in his father's footsteps. What was he like? Chapter 29 of 2 Chronicles reveals several godly qualities the young king possessed. To begin with, as C. E. Autrey has insightfully pointed out,* he proved to be a man of tenacious purpose. At last Israel had a leader who would lead,

---

*See C. E. Autrey, *Revivals in the Old Testament,* (Grand Rapids: Zondervan Publishing House, 1960).

one who would not simply be carried along in the flow. He proved to be a stalwart, courageous, unbending leader. Hezekiah himself said, "It is in mine heart to make a covenant with the LORD God of Israel" (2 Chronicles 29:10, KJV). Revival invariably begins there; a deep resolve to enter into an agreement with God to love, serve, and obey Him at all costs. Leaders like that are vital to securing God's blessings. How desperately we need leaders who will lead. Little dedication means little blessings, for the "Holy Spirit . . . God has given to *those who obey him*" (Acts 5:32). Hezekiah grew into a man of determined purpose; he would obey God at any cost and keep the covenant.

Secondly, the young king honestly faced the reality of Israel's spiritual situation and became a man of action. Prayer for revival is vital and foundational, but it takes action also. The Bible tells us that Hezekiah "in the *first* year of his reign, in the *first* month, opened the doors of the house of the LORD" (2 Chronicles 29:3, KJV). At the very outset he grasped the fact that worship plays an important part when God begins to turn a people to himself. The psalmist said God inhabits "the praise of Israel" (Psalm 22:3). It was in dynamic worship that God gave the Moravians their profound awakening. That principle can be illustrated endless times throughout Scripture and history. So the king immediately took the situation in hand, acted, and instituted temple worship, which his spiritually benighted father had stopped.

Thirdly, Hezekiah embodied insight and wisdom. He did not make the tragic blunder of his royal ancestor Rehoboam when he ascended the throne of his father Solomon and rejected the advice of the wise elders. That error cost young Rehoboam the kingdom. But not Hezekiah; "He brought in the priests and the Levites, and gathered them together" (2 Chronicles 29:4, KJV). He realized he needed others to help bring about the necessary reforms. That demonstrated wisdom, especially for a zealous young ruler of only twenty-five years of age. None can dispense with the help, advice, and aid of others. Failing to grasp that reality has run many a revival on the rocks.

Finally, Hezekiah radiated integrity and zeal: "He did that which was right in the sight of the LORD, according to all that David his father had done" (2 Chronicles 29:2, KJV). It was his sincere love for the Lord that endued him with integrity and zeal. In New Testament language, he was a man filled with the Holy Spirit (Ephesians 5:18). Thus God had in hand through this young prophet-king an instrument whom He could powerfully use.

It is always the same. The "prophets" God raises up for revival are people of purpose, action, wisdom, integrity, and zeal. And whether it is Hezekiah in the eighth century B.C., Zinzendorf of the eighteenth century A.D., or us today, God uses people with those qualities.

The pieces are now in place, there is a godly leader who will lead, and the God of hope is ready to act and revive His people.

The Revival and Its Dynamics

The awakening shed its first faint flash of hopeful light when God opened the shades of Hezekiah's mind to see the urgency of the nation's needs. Unless a sense of urgency can be generated, revival never comes. Concern conceives revival. Hezekiah saw the need—his walk with God wrought that.

Note how the king took the matter in hand. He started his reform at the real heart of the issue: the *spiritual need* of Judah. Being in a position to wield political power, he could have forced a superficial reform. That has often been tried, but with little lasting results. Hezekiah wielded his influence where true revival always begins, with the spiritual deadness of the people. Professor Kaiser points out that God set four choices before the king. He tells us:

> Each one is a call to turn from wickedness and sin, as that programmatic verse of 2 Chronicles 7:14 specified. The four *alternatives* are:
> 1. Turn to Him with an unqualified trust, or He will not turn to us (v. 6).
> 2. Turn to Him with a wholehearted obedience, or He will make us despicable to all (v. 7).
> 3. Turn to Him with glad service, or He will not turn His anger from us (v. 8).
> 4. Turn to Him with unceasing prayer, or He will withdraw His presence and favor from us (v. 9).[3]

Hezekiah made the right choices. He turned to God with all his heart. Then, the young king undertook a nationwide return to the Lord: First, as already seen, he opened the house of God. Then he gathered the priests and Levites and gave them instructions: "Hear me, Levites! Now sanctify yourselves, and sanctify the house of the LORD, the God of your fathers, and carry out the filth from the holy place" (2 Chronicles 29:5, RSV). If the religious leaders do not get thoroughly right with God and be personally revived, what hope is there for the people? Leaders are duty bound to seek fervently God's face, "sanctify themselves," and "carry out the filth from the holy place." That principle applies to every age.

The Cambuslang Awakening

In the great Cambuslang Revival of the 1840s, the movement started because of the fervent seeking of God's face by William McCulloch, pastor and leader of the little congregation in Cambuslang, a small community a short distance from Glasgow, Scotland. That burdened leader became the key that unlocked the storehouse of glory, ushering in a marvelous spiritual awakening.

McCulloch fell under deep conviction of the dire need of renewal in his beloved congregation. At the same time, nearby, John Welsh, a devout Scot and profound man of prayer, experienced a deepening of his prayer life. He began interceding eight hours out of every twenty-four, often spending days and nights in fasting and prayers for revival. It was reported of him, "On the coldest winter nights . . . he hath been found lying on the ground weeping, and wrestling with the Lord. . . . Overcharged with grief, he told his wife he had that to press him which she had not, the souls of 3000 to answer for, whilst he knew not how it was with many of them."[4] That is the "Spirit of prayer" that only the Holy Spirit can produce. For that burden, we should earnestly seek God.

With the beginning of that profound Spirit of prayer and the devoted seeking of God's face, it is little surprise that societies for prayer sprang up spontaneously everywhere. Cambuslang in particular became one of the centers for the prayer groups that started flourishing. When William McCulloch came to Cambuslang as pastor in 1731, three prayer societies were already functioning. By 1742, when the revival began, the number had increased to a dozen or more. Thus God set the stage for one of His mighty miracles.

On January 31, 1742, McCulloch preached on 2 Corinthians 1:3–4: "Blessed be the God and Father of our Lord Jesus Christ, the Father of mercies and God of all comfort, who comforts us in all our affliction, so that we may be able to comfort those who are in any affliction, with the comfort with which we ourselves are comforted by God" (RSV). That date seems to pinpoint the initial moment when the curtain came up on act one of the drama of revival. A deep thirst for the things of God began to sweep the entire parched community. Conviction took hold of many. By February 14, the church was overflowing with people seeking Christ, many standing for want of seats. In after-meetings, people wept in anguish of soul, crying out for salvation. The awakening was under way.

Crowds soon flocked to Cambuslang from all quarters. One of the first in southern England to hear the news of the revival was George Whitefield. Many urged him to come to Scotland. A friend wrote from the Glasgow area, "O, Mr. Whitefield. Why are you so long a coming to poor Scotland again? How many say, 'When is he coming?' For the Lord's sake do not lay aside thoughts of coming, whatever work you may have in England."[5] Whitefield could not resist that, and when he arrived, the full blessings of God arrived with him.

On Tuesday, July 6, 1742, Whitefield rode into Cambuslang. He preached at two o'clock in the afternoon and at six and nine that same night. The power of the Holy Spirit fell upon him, for Whitefield himself said, "Such a commotion surely never was heard of, especially . . . at night. It far out-did all that I ever saw in America."[6] Many moaned like "wounded soldiers." Whitefield related that all night, out in the open fields, one could hear the agonizing groans of the convicted, as well as the voice of praise from those who had found forgiveness in Christ.

Whitefield preached to as many as 20,000 people in the open air, as was his style. He declared, "Scarce ever was such a sight seen in Scotland."[7] On one occasion he preached for an hour and a half to an enraptured multitude on Isaiah 54:4: "Fear not, for you will not be ashamed; be not confounded, for you will not be put to shame; for you will forget the shame of your youth, and the reproach of your widowhood you will remember no more" (RSV). Hundreds came to Christ in that small town of Cambuslang. When real revival breaks out it becomes incredibly attractive.

The high-water mark of the flood tide came at a communion service. Whitefield declared, "Such a passover has not been heard of."[8] Only heaven can accurately record the conversions. The great preacher testified that this became the greatest single service he had ever seen. John Erskine wrote about the awakening, "It is to be hoped that the work will not only go through our land in the length of it and breadth of it, but spread from kingdom to kingdom till the kingdoms of the earth shall become the kingdom of God and of His Christ."[9] He was hardly disappointed. Reports of the awakening at Cambuslang spread rapidly throughout the country and overseas. In America the First Great Awakening moved up and down the East Coast. McCulloch had established correspondence with Jonathan Edwards concerning the centrality of prayer that helped spread the revival significantly. They aided each other in their respective movements. It takes leaders.

The Jews experienced a similar renewal under Hezekiah. After the king had called the leaders together, he next confessed sins. He acknowledged the iniquities of the fathers, *and their own* (2 Chronicles 29:6ff). Confession and cleansing lie at the heart of a true awakening. Moreover, Hezekiah correctly pointed out the certainty of God's judgment because of their sin: "Therefore the wrath of the LORD came on Judah and Jerusalem, and he has made them an object of horror" (2 Chronicles 29:8, RSV).

Important to note is the fact that the confession was very specific and pointed. The king acknowledged they had "shut up the doors of the house of the LORD," had "put out the lamps," and had not "burned incense" (2 Chronicles 29:7). "Shutting the doors" meant that worship and praise to God had ceased. "Putting out the lamps" typifies the curtailing of the light of God's Word. Spiritual depression always follows hard on the heels of an absence of proclamation. Biblical preaching, teaching, and witnessing are vital to dynamic spirituality. Suppress or pervert the Word of God and you suppress the Spirit's working, who alone creates faith through the Word (Romans 10:17). The curtailment of "burning the incense" speaks of the absence of prayer. That typology consistently surfaces throughout the Scriptures. Israel's leaders had plunged the dagger deep in the back of vital religion. Hezekiah became God's physician to heal the wound.

This tragic situation had grown out of the Jew's "unfaithfulness" and the fact that they had "turned away their faces from the habitation of the LORD" (2 Chronicles 29:6). Something had to be done. So Hezekiah, as their leader, began by confession. He first confessed his own sins, then the sins of the people. In that he did the right thing, as any spiritual leader should. Never has there been a revival that did not erupt in honest, open, specific confession of sins—one's own iniquities and those of society generally. Both aspects of confession become central in a biblical awakening.

But some instruction is often needed on the point of confession of sins as it relates to revival. John, in his First Epistle, presents the guidelines when he states: "If we confess our sins, he is faithful and just, and will forgive our sins and cleanse us from all unrighteousness" (1 John 1:9, RSV). The intriguing implications of the word *confess* speaks to the present. In the language of the New Testament, it is a compound word. John wedded two different words, and the union gave birth to a new, rich truth. The term is comprised of the verb *to say* and the prefix *the same*. Thus the word we translate "confess" in our English Bibles literally means "to say the same thing as" or "to assent to" or "to agree with." Confession literally means we "agree with" concerning our sins.

With whom, however, do we agree concerning our iniquity? The answer is obvious: the Holy Spirit (John 16:7–11). He is the One who points out our sins in the first place. Therefore, to confess sins scripturally is "to concede to" or "to agree with" the convicting Spirit of God that some *particular* act of rebellion *truly is a sin*. It means to get out of one's own self and stand with the Holy Spirit, be objective about the issue, and agree with Him. Confession centers in an objective standing with God against one's specific sins as well as those of society generally, and not in merely rationalizing them away or finding superficial excuses.

This principle and practice precludes any sort of general, nonspecific confession of sins. For example, how often we simply pray, "Lord, forgive me of all my sins!" This is not the way the Bible teaches a Christian should confess iniquities; hence, probably the reason so little assurance of forgiveness is found. Such an approach to confession may be fitting for a worship service or in a group, but in individual private prayer, this will never do. To confess sins, according to John, means naming them specifically and individually, agreeing with the Spirit of God that the particular act of which He convicts truly is a sin. No one commits sin as an indefinable whole; thus, the confession of sin should not be done in an indefinable manner. Each sin should be confessed one by one and named for what it is. After all, sins were committed one by one. They were individual acts of rebellion. This principle necessitates lingering long before God, long enough to permit the Holy Spirit to search one out, convict of sin, and place His finger on those particular deeds that constitute evil and have grieved Him.

Perhaps a personal experience here will give some insight to the personal sin situation. On one occasion a retired missionary spoke in our church. Her challenge centered on confession. In the course of her message, she urged us to make out what she called a "sin account." She instructed us to take some paper and write down several numbers in sequence in the left-hand column. Then in the quiet of a secret place before God, we were to pray that the Holy Spirit would reveal every single act displeasing to God, thus marring our fellowship with Jesus Christ. Next, she urged us to write down those specific sins that we had never individually brought before Him in prior confession. When we could think of nothing more that had grieved God, she challenged us to bring the wonderful promise of 1 John 1:9 to each issue.

Many of us took the challenge. I made out my personal "sin account." Even though I had known this principle for some years and had attempted to live by it, much to my humbling, the Spirit of God brought to my mind many unconfessed sins. The probing finger of God brought back to my mind sins I had committed months, even years ago: sins I had never really brought before God. The Holy Spirit searched me out. Then I claimed the promise of forgiveness in 1 John 1:9. Of course, confession means *forsaking* sins as well as acknowledging them. That goes without saying. If we love God we do not love sin, nor continue in it.

Now, that spiritual exercise was not mere morbid introspection. It was simple honesty before God and with myself. Therefore, it brought instant forgiveness and joy. The forgiveness of God is a marvelous experience indeed. New liberty, love, and joy are released. Nor is that liberating joy just superficial emotionalism. "Where the Spirit of the Lord is, there is freedom" (2 Corinthians 3:17). True praise and joy follow as the natural expression in knowing Christ and His forgiveness.

A beautiful illustration of this principle of joy abounded in the life and ministry of Billy Bray, a "revived" Welsh preacher of the last century. He was a happy man in Christ. His biographer relates the following incident:

> I remember taking a walk with him early one morning, when his conversation was of heaven. He stopped, as if a thought had suddenly occurred to him. He remained silent for a moment with uplifted eyes, which almost immediately filled with tears; a "Praise the Lord!" escaped his lips and, though an old man, he bounded away like a hart or deer. When I came up to him he was praising the Lord aloud, as if it was the business of his life, and said, "My dear brother, if I only lived to my privilege, I should not feel the ground over which I walk."
>
> At a district meeting held at Hicks' Mill, in 1866, Mr. Oliver, in describing the triumphant death of a woman, said she died shouting "Victory." This touched Billy's heart, and he shouted "Glory! If a *dying* woman praised the Lord, I should think a *living* man might."[10]

Revived, cleansed people are happy people. They truly have "joy unspeakable and full of glory" (1 Peter 1:8, KJV). Burns states that an awakening "leaves in its wake numberless happy men and women whose faces are aglow with a new light." Forgiveness fills the heart with praise, for God has committed himself; if we confess our sins, He is *faithful* (faithful to His promise and His attribute of love) and *just* (Christ bore on the cross the full penalty of our sins) to forgive us of our rebellion and cleanse us from *all unrighteousness.* "To forgive" in John's terminology means to wipe out a debt. To be "cleansed" implies the blotting out of a stain. God will not only eradicate all debts, He will even blot out the stain of the memory that may drag one down into spiritual depression and guilt feelings. God forgets (Jeremiah 31:34), so can we. That is true liberty and unspeakable joy.

The blood of Christ proves powerful and precious beyond words. What a reviving experience it is when one comes before God with honest, broken confession. Although some may condemn the exercise as unhealthy, negative introspection, such is not the case at all. *Honesty* becomes the keynote. And that brings about a new fellowship with God. Life glows. Remember, the "joy of the Lord" constitutes a real part of real revival. So, if we want a spiritual awakening, personal, and corporate, it all begins by making out one's personal "sin account."

A second principle immediately emerges at this point. What if some sins involve relationships with others as well as one's relationship to God? In such an instance, merely to confess those sins to God alone proves insufficient to experience the full freedom of Christ's forgiveness. We should confess them to God, to be sure, but in the Sermon on the Mount, Jesus stated: "So if you are offering your gift at the altar, and there remember that your brother has something against you, leave your gift there before the altar and go; first be reconciled to your brother, and then come and offer your gift" (Matthew 5:23–24, RSV). If one sins against another person and fellowship becomes marred, restitution must be made to the offended person as well as to God.

The first time the Holy Spirit bore this truth home to my life took place several years ago while serving as pastor in a small church in Fort Worth, Texas. A young, deeply spiritual man preached powerfully on this theme in our congregation. The Spirit of God profoundly probed all of us. Many were compelled by the Holy Spirit to put things right with various people. I, too, had to acknowledge, much to my chagrin, that I had sinned against several individuals. To be honest with God and myself, I knew I should put those things right. If I were to have real peace and live a revived life, I had to follow God's lead.

The experience was anything but easy; pride dies hard. The Holy Spirit normally must bring us to a place of brokenness before God (Psalm 51:17) before we find ourselves willing to be humbled before others (James 4:10). But it brings inner peace, and only the broken heart can be molded and formed into the kind of revived, joyous life that will exemplify Jesus Christ. He,

94

too, was a man meek and lowly in heart (Matthew 11:29, KJV).

A final implication of the confession of sin centers around the fact that there can even be times when sin manifests itself not simply against God alone or against another single individual; it may be open, flagrant, and known to others. Does the Bible say anything on this score? James tells us, "Therefore confess your sins to one another, and pray for one another, that you may be healed" (James 5:16, RSV). If one's sins are so gross and open that reproach comes upon the church, and thus the fellowship of the church is ruptured, then forgiveness should obviously be sought from the entire congregation. This principle lies behind the scriptural practice of church discipline, a practice that many congregations have seemingly forgotten today. Furthermore, this is probably the real scriptural meaning of a public "rededication." Sin precipitates the need for rededication; therefore, if one's sins are open and reproachful, they should be confessed and made right with God and the church. Hezekiah certainly openly confessed the sins of the people. But make no mistake, open confession is painfully difficult. It is not a mere "airing of one's dirty linen" before the world. It emerges out of real brokenness. Moreover, there should be that understanding person or group in the fellowship of believers with whom we can be open, honest, and candid about ourselves.

A Word of Caution

Let it be said that care must be taken. This openness should never be allowed to degenerate into a display of one's sin before the whole world just for the sake of display. Some have fallen into this demonic trap. Such an exercise can become very damaging to spiritual health and fellowship. Nor, as pointed out earlier, should we engage in a morbid inner search to dredge up old sins. Such introspection does not bring about spiritual health; rather, it precipitates spiritual sickness. Moreover, there are some areas of our lives about which only God should ever know. Some sins are never to be revealed to others. Yet at the same time, the need remains for honest openness among God's people. The basic principle centers in the truth that sin should be confessed in the area of offense, and fellowship thereby restored. As the Holy Spirit develops a sensitivity among the company of believers, He will grant wisdom so that it will be clear what should be shared and with whom (James 1:5). One would hope that our churches would be revived and thus grow in love, understanding, and healing.

The real purpose of confession, as implied, centers in the fact that it keeps intact the foundations of Christian fellowship, *koinonia*. John employs this gripping word throughout the first chapter of his First epistle. It denotes a vital, living fellowship and relationship where two parties walk together in harmony, understanding, and love. Every church should be a dynamic fellowship of love and acceptance, with God and with one another. If it is not, it needs an awakening.

Thus, when God's people experience His forgiveness, and true cleansing comes, *real* hope for revival emerges on the horizon. Remember, God is "hope" in revival; therefore, we need to "seek His face." Hezekiah and Israel learned that basic truth.

The Covenant

After the proper confession of sins and receiving the gracious forgiveness of God, Hezekiah committed himself to a covenant: "Now it is in my heart to make a covenant with the LORD" (2 Chronicles 29:10, RSV). Covenant commitment always follows as the natural outcome of cleansing. As invariably seen, in revival there must be dedication. A spirit of surrender by cleansed Christians always precedes a mighty outpouring of the Holy Spirit, even if the number is few. No full giving of one's self means no lasting revival. Therefore, leading the way to commitment, Hezekiah urged the leaders: "My sons, do not now be negligent, for the LORD has chosen you to stand in his presence to minister to him, and to be his ministers and burn incense to him" (2 Chronicles 29:11, RSV). And who is worthy to stand in the presence of the Lord and minister? The psalmist answered, "He that hath clean hands, and a pure heart" (Psalm 24:4, KJV). Cleansing and covenant commitment are intertwined in an awakening, as young King Hezekiah discovered.

With that depth of dedication the whole nation now hovered on the edge of a general awakening. Then the king arranged a large and significant worship service. In the setting of worship Hezekiah re-instituted the sin offering, the burnt offering, and the thank offering. In that, the pattern of revival emerges.

The worship started where it ought to start, with the sin offering. As seen, cleansing and forgiveness come first. Note that the offering was made for "the kingdom, and for the sanctuary, and for Judah" (2 Chronicles 29:21, KJV). "The kingdom" meant the king's house found forgiveness. "The sanctuary" spoke to the cleansing of the priesthood. The priests then received "the blood, and sprinkled it on the altar" (2 Chronicles 29:22, KJV). In Judah the entire nation was "washed in the blood."

Dr. Wilbur M. Smith points out that this was the first time in over eight hundred years* that "blood" is referred to as part of the sacrifice offered by the Israelites.[11] Blood is mentioned in the biblical records during that protracted period, but not in connection with sacrifice. Further, in the Hezekiah revival, the blood was not just sprinkled upon the altar with the finger, as in the Law (Leviticus 4:17); it was literally dashed against the altar. They deeply sensed their need of forgiveness.

Then, "they laid their hands upon" the sacrificial goat. By this symbol the priests typified the transferal of the sins to the sacrifice. The goat became the sin offering, and the people experienced reconciliation with God. This act obviously finds its full and contemporary reality in Jesus Christ who became our sin offering. "For he hath made him to be sin for us, who knew no sin; that we might be made the righteousness of God in him" (2 Corinthians 5:21, KJV).

Hezekiah then sacrificed the burnt offering for the whole of the nation. Fire and burning points to purification. The offering became an expression of the people's purity and consecration. Now cleansed and consecrated, they began to sing the songs of the Lord. They sang and played "with the instruments of David" (2 Chronicles 29:26). It must have been a time of great rejoicing. That is always true of revival. Churches do not know real joy until the "joy of the Lord" comes mightily upon them. It is not surprising the revived people then "bowed themselves and worshiped" (2 Chronicles 29:29). They literally prostrated themselves before God as He revealed himself as hope for the future.

---

*With one exception, which was insincere and unscriptural.

Finally, the thank offering was given. The people gladly responded with such gladness and abundance there were not enough priests to administer the ritual (2 Chronicles 29:34). When God's people share in true revival, no one needs to urge, beg, and plead with them to do their duty. Glad generosity overflows from a revived "willing heart" (2 Chronicles 29:31). And what was the natural outcome for the awakened people of God? "The service of the house of the LORD was restored. And Hezekiah and all the people rejoiced because of what God had done for the people; for the thing came about suddenly" (2 Chronicles 29:35–36, RSV). The "suddenly" of verse 36 is much akin to the "suddenly" of Acts 2:2, when the Holy Spirit suddenly fell on the Day of Pentecost. Revival often comes from this God of revealing hope "suddenly." O for a "suddenly" to occur in our day, in our lives!

Redemption and Revival

But that wonderful sacrificial worship did not constitute the final climax of the revival. After all the sacrifices were offered, they celebrated the Passover. As often pointed out, that significant religious exercise spoke of God's redemptive work; in Israel's case, freedom from Egyptian bondage. Our experience of redemption centers in salvation through Jesus Christ. To put the Passover in contemporary terms, as Jesus did in the institution of the Lord's Supper, it speaks of redemption and new life. Several evangelistic principles of spiritual awakening can be discovered in this observance of the Passover that Hezekiah instituted (2 Chronicles 30).

Note initially that "all Israel" was invited (2 Chronicles 30:5). The king wanted every straying Israelite, not just those of Judah, to revel in the power and presence of the redemptive God. "Go into all the world," Jesus said. Hezekiah made his proclamation in that spirit. The call to the wayward had four elements of appeal:

First, the prophetic call to "return to the LORD, the God of Abraham, Isaac and Israel" (2 Chronicles 30:6) sounded forth. The call to salvation rests at the heart of an awakening (Acts 2:40).

Secondly, they were urged to shun the path of their fathers

who had strayed and forgotten God and thus suffered judgment (2 Chronicles 30:7). That constitutes the essence of repentance (Acts 2:38).

Thirdly, the king urged them to "yield . . . to the LORD" (2 Chronicles 30:8). Surrender and revival are virtually synonymous (Acts 16:31).

Fourthly, Israel heard the admonition to "come to the sanctuary" (2 Chronicles 30:8). God wants worship (John 4:23). After all, it behooves mere creatures to worship the Creator. This mandate rests upon all. And when one comes to salvation, adoration and praise become a natural expression of the new life in Christ (Acts 2:42).

A positive response would insure God's forgiveness, mercy, and grace. When God revives the land, an immediate appeal comes to those who are lost and outside the covenant. God wants to make them citizens of His kingdom. Revival magnifies Passover principles as those without Christ are evangelized. "For the LORD . . . is gracious and merciful, and will not turn away his face from you" (2 Chronicles 30:9, KJV).

The People's Response

Hezekiah's clarion call received a mixed response, as it usually does. Some heard the appeal and "scorned and ridiculed them" (2 Chronicles 30:10). That destructive, negative reaction can be expected. Sadly, there will be those who reject God's call to salvation, and then attempt to justify their rebellion with ridicule. But remember, ridicule is the weapon of weakness. Gratefully, however, not all responded in that fashion. "A few men of the Northern Kingdom humbled themselves and came to Jerusalem" (2 Chronicles 30:11, RSV). Thank God for those humble few. But on Judah, the Spirit's effectual call was especially evident: "The hand of God was upon Judah to give them one heart to do what the king and the princes commanded by the word of the LORD" (2 Chronicles 30:12, RSV). That threefold response is typical of a spiritual awakening: scorn, a few seekers, and then those whom God profoundly touches. Why? The answer rests in the elective sovereignty of God. Simply put, the sovereign "hand of God . . . upon Judah to give them one heart."

Yet, one thing remains certain, God will redeem *all* who will come to Him.

So, regardless of the scorn and indifference on the part of many, "a very great assembly" gathered (2 Chronicles 30:13). And what happened? They eradicated all false gods (2 Chronicles 30:14) and observed the Passover. The lamb was slain and the blood sprinkled on the altar. They learned in dramatic fashion:

There is a fountain filled with blood
Drawn from Immanuel's veins;
And sinners, plunged beneath that flood,
Lose all their guilty stains.

Redemption had come. And even though some irregularities occurred, Hezekiah prayed and God graciously heard. He knew God had revealed himself as hope in revival, so he set "his heart on seeking God" (2 Chronicles 30:19). The result: God "healed the people" (2 Chronicles 30:20). The God of hope had met their seeking of His face and significantly supplied their needs.

It is easy to understand why "great gladness" (2 Chronicles 30:21) and fourteen days of festival followed. The redemptive God had come among them and caused great rejoicing. Nothing gladdens God's people like the redemption of the lost and straying. Seeing a great number saved, in itself, often revives believers.

Moreover, the people received instructions in the Word of God (30:22). The proclamation of the Word becomes a vital ingredient in any spiritual awakening. The preaching of Isaiah, Hosea, and Micah, contemporaries of Hezekiah, no doubt made a significant contribution to the spirit of revival that swept the land.

The results of the awakening were astounding. Four significant spiritual steps were taken:

1. Idols were destroyed (2 Chronicles 31:1). Throughout the land the revived people marched, obliterating every false god and idol. They demonstrated their repentance in a real way.

2. Public worship was restored. Judah received a new heart for God. Revival fills the houses of worship. Low churchmanship means low Christianity which means low life. In the Welsh Revival of 1904–1906, the churches burst with people twenty-

four hours a day, seven days a week. Why do seeming multitudes stay away from our churches today? A short time ago, a major denomination in America conducted a widespread survey to find out. They received many reasons, but two causes were given everywhere: (1) The pastor's sermons are dull, and (2) The services are lifeless. What an indictment! But how different when revival comes; everything changes. Pastors and church members no longer need to cajole people to "come to church," they can hardly be driven away.

3. And perhaps most important of all, the people of God began to live holy lives (2 Chronicles 30:15–20). We must never forget, without holiness "no one will see the Lord" (Hebrews 12:14). It is beautiful to see a truly holy life. In the midst of sin and sensuality, a holy life stands out like a bright star in a dark sky. A true spiritual awakening means a revival of holiness.

4. National prosperity followed (2 Chronicles 32:27). History tells us continually that national well-being becomes one of the blessed beneficiaries of an awakening. The psalmist knew this: "Blessed is the nation whose God is the LORD" (Psalm 33:12, KJV).

Of course, one central question immediately emerges again: Can we expect God to do that sort of reviving work in our day? Remember, our Lord is "the same yesterday, today, and forever" (Hebrews 13:8). It can happen any time. For example, longing for revival permeated a number of Christians in Bridgehampton, Long Island in 1799. They grew deeply concerned about the spiritual situation in their church and community. The cause of Christ languished. They longed for the grace of God. In April they began to meet weekly for special prayer. They continued meeting faithfully through the summer, although they had no special or visible encouragement. But they persevered. God waits on those who will intercede until the heavens are heavy with stored-up blessings. Finally, they prevailed, and God did open heaven and answered their prayers with a great revival that lasted all winter and into the next spring. The pastor, Rev. Aaron Woolworth, reported:

> God hath shown himself a prayer-hearing God, and exhibited a sufficient reason why His people, even in the darkest seasons, should perseveringly wait upon Him in the

way of His own appointment. In due time, they may be confident of reaping, if they faint not.[12]

Conclusion

So take courage! There is hope. We can legitimately expect a fresh awakening in our contemporary moment. Under Hezekiah God revealed himself as *hope*. He always does. Therefore, may this God of hope grant reviving grace, motivating us to "seek His face."

Where's the Glow?

In a Spiritual Awakening God Reveals Himself as

HOLY

Therefore, "Turn from Your Wicked Ways."
EXODUS 32–34

Introduction

"If thy Presence will not go with us, do not carry us up from here" (Exodus 33:15, RSV), cried an anguished Moses. He seemingly teetered at the end of his tether. But then, life as God's leader never promised to be a smooth road. The Lord's path often teams with trials.

It is not surprising that Moses had a difficult time in being a leader. Look at the rebellious Israelites whom he had been leading: complaining, griping, blaming their leaders; not satisfied with manna, they had to have meat, even longing for the "fleshpots of Egypt." The culmination of their waywardness came when Moses scaled Mount Sinai to receive the glorious Law of the Covenant. In his absence they broke loose into idolatry, immorality, gluttony, and drunkenness. And they even blamed Moses for it all. What a situation! But then, that's what sin will do. Charles H. Spurgeon hit the mark when he said:

> Think of the havoc which the tyrant, sin, has made of our natural estate and heritage. Eden is withered—its very site is forgotten. Our restfulness among the trees of the field, freely yielding their fruit is gone and God hath said, "In the sweat of thy face shalt thou eat bread." The field we till has lost its spontaneous yield of corn: "Thorns also and thistles shall it bring forth to thee." Our life has lost its glory and immortality; for "Dust thou art, and unto dust shalt thou return." Every woman in her pangs of travail, every man in his weariness of labour, and all of us together in the grief of death, see what sin has done for us as to our mortal bodies. Alas, it has gone deeper: It has ruined our souls. Sin has unmanned man. The crown and glory of his manhood it has thrown to the ground. All our faculties are out of gear; all our tendencies are perverted.[1]

And in Israel's case, these sinners were supposed to be the holy people of a holy God. Moses' plaintive cry to Yahweh is understandable.

Right at that moment, however, it seems as if a faint ray of hopeful light flickered at the far end of Moses' dark, depressing tunnel—almost imperceptible, but there. Hear him pray again: "I pray thee, if I have found favor in thy sight, show me now thy ways, that I may know thee and find favor in thy sight," (Exodus 33:13, RSV). Then from the depths of his heart Moses pleaded, "I pray thee, show me thy glory" (Exodus 33:18, RSV). "Let me just see *You*, LORD, for all *You* are!" begged God's servant. Moses actually asked to see the essence of the Holy God of Glory. He knew if he could catch that vision, he could persevere to the end.

God graciously replied, "You cannot see my face; for man shall not see me and live" (Exodus 33:20, RSV). Moses did not quite understand that to behold the face of God in His holy glory would mean being liquidated more quickly than dropping an ice cube in a cauldron of molten steel. But this holy, yet gracious God said, "Moses, I have heard you, I will make all my goodness—my consuming holiness—pass before you."

Moses may well have replied in astonishment, "But how can that be?" God said to His dejected, depressed yet hopeful servant:

> Behold, there is a place by me where you shall stand upon the rock; and while my glory passes by I will put you in a cleft of the rock, and I will cover you with my hand until I have passed by; then I will take away my hand, and you shall see my back; [as I depart in the Shekinah cloud of my holy glory] (Exodus 33:21–23, RSV).

To see God, if only the "after-glow," must have been an incredible experience for Moses. But we sing about it too:

> He hideth my soul in the cleft of the Rock
> That shadows a dry, thirsty land;
> He hideth my life in the depths of his love,
> And covers me there with his hand.

106

It all came to pass exactly as God promised. Moses caught a glimpse of the glorious holiness of God, if only a backward, fleeting vision. Now completely refreshed, revived, and ready to lead, Moses returned to the camp. But when the Israelites saw him, they shrank back in fear. For though Moses knew it not, the skin of his face literally glowed from that afterglow glimpse of the God who "is light and in him is no darkness at all" (1 John 1:5, RSV). That's holiness, and that's revival!

In a true awakening, God *always* reveals himself as *holy*. A revival invariably reveals the "Shekinah." God has said, "I will show myself holy among those who are near me, and before all the people I will be glorified" (Leviticus 10:3, RSV). Revival ground is "holy ground." Therefore, we *must* "take off our shoes" and "turn from our wicked ways," as our theme text admonishes. The consuming holiness of God demands such.

This revival principle Paul stressed when he wrote the Corinthians, "We all, with unveiled face, beholding the glory of the Lord, are being changed into his likeness from one degree of glory to another" (2 Corinthians 3:18, RSV). A spiritual awakening is no more than God's people seeing God in His holiness, turning from their wicked ways, and being transformed into His likeness.

Israel surely stood in need of a touch from God as Moses had experienced. Even though they were the Lord's redeemed, they desperately needed to see God in His holiness. They were in a far worse *spiritual* desert than the hot, dry, miserable sands at the foot of Mt. Sinai where they had pitched their tents. They had broken the covenant almost the moment they received it. But right there, in the midst of rebellion, God often steps in and mightily revives His own. He is merciful beyond comprehension. Moses' and Israel's experience as recorded in Exodus 32–34 present a perfect pattern of this gracious revival principle at work. As one commentator put it, the event is "an excellent study in rebellion and apostasy, restoration of the Lord's purpose, and the renewal of covenant life."[2] Several revival realities surge through the turbulent story.

When any people are awakened to the holy, covenant-restoring God, as we have stressed before, they inevitably discover first of all their own sin.

God's Holiness in Revival Highlights Human Iniquity

After all is said and done, the bottom line of the human predicament is sin. Our iniquities, blinding us to God, causes His countenance to fade away. Sin alone blurs the divine vision, then all of life slips out of joint. This rebellion against God exerts itself, without exception, in three distinct areas of experience, just as in Israel's case on the slopes of Sinai.

Initially, iniquity manifests itself in *ingratitude*. Hear the thankless, thoughtless Jews: "As for this Moses . . ." (Exodus 32:1). They almost exude contempt against God's instrument in the Exodus. Although Moses had just led them from their cruel Egyptian bondage, they displayed disdain for God's agent in that wonderful deliverance. What ingratitude! Moses had forsaken the luxury of Pharaoh's palace for them (Exodus 2:11–15). He finally found a home in Midian, but then he left the security of his father-in-law's tent to care for the Israelites (Exodus 4:18). He had courageously and successfully stood down Pharaoh (Exodus 12:31–32). Moses was God's man in multiplied miracles. He had led them to freedom, parted the Red Sea, and provided manna and water. The Jews' reaction? "As for this Moses!" How ungracious!

Underlying it all, however, there lurked a basic ingratitude toward God; Moses moved among them as no more than God's channel of blessings. It was actually God they held in contempt for not providing all they craved and lusted after. They were utterly selfish. Such a lifestyle falls far from wisdom—and becomes destructive of all that is good. As Paul wrote, "Claiming to be wise, they became fools, and exchanged the glory of the immortal God for images resembling mortal man or birds or animals or reptiles. Therefore God gave them up in the lusts of their hearts to impurity, to the dishonoring of their bodies among themselves, because they exchanged the truth about God for a lie and worshiped and served the creature rather than the Creator, who is blessed forever! Amen" (Romans 1:22–25, RSV). All sin essentially strikes out against God. Rebellion against His authority rests at the core of all human wickedness.

The Israelites' attitude reads very similar to a chronicle of today's society. Has there ever been a more malcontent, self-centered, sensual, violent generation than at the present moment? This discontent has extended to every segment of society, even at times and in some respects to us who profess to be Christians. It seems to manifest itself in the attitude that we do not want to hear anything negative or what might expose sin and judgment. "Be positive" is the cry—even in many churches. Much in the Christian experience is positive, to be sure. But true negative realities must be faced as well if we are to be mature and realistic. Let us be positive, yes, but let us also be true to God, His Word, and ourselves. But too often we act just like the Israelites. It appears we are always looking for greener pastures. To find a truly contented person today is not as easy as it would appear. Some believers do not even seem satisfied with God's clear will. This clamoring for more and more, better and better, indicates the need for real revival.

Further, human iniquity reveals itself in *irreverence*. Hear the Jews: "As for this Moses . . . we do not know what has become of him" (Exodus 32:1, RSV). That was not true; they knew Moses had ascended the Holy Mount to appear before God. The Scripture states:

> Then Moses went up on the mountain, and the cloud covered the mountain. The glory of the LORD settled on Mount Sinai, and the cloud covered it six days; and on the seventh day he called to Moses out of the midst of the cloud. Now the appearance of the glory of the LORD was like a devouring fire on the top of the mountain in the sight of the people of Israel. And Moses entered the cloud, and went up on the mountain. And Moses was on the mountain forty days and forty nights (Exodus 24:15–18, RSV).

The Israelites clearly saw Moses enter the cloud—the cloud was still there with its unearthly glow. They beheld the brilliant lightning and heard the rumbling thunder—it still echoed. What did they mean, "As for this Moses . . . we do not know what has become of him"? They knew Moses was up there meeting with God. So what if it had been forty days since he left the camp below, what is that before the holy God? Some of them in their worldly shortsightedness probably cynically said, "Moses is up there on some holy trip." The Israelites irreverently ignored the presence of God shrouding the holy mount. Their indifference seems incredible. But one of the cardinal temptations of believers is to develop a deadening familiarity with the sublime. That attitude will invariably result in irreverence. Actually, sin will always in some manner reduce itself to irreverence toward the work and Word of God. Then life gets all out of balance. Acknowledging God and putting Him in His proper reverential position keeps life in balanced perspective. Israel, however, stood condemned.

Finney's Revival

That sort of resistance to God's holy workings must be exposed and rooted out if spiritual awakening is to come. Charles G. Finney learned the lesson in the early days of his itinerant revival ministry. After great victories in Jefferson County, New York, Finney's first work, he began to expand his horizons. He felt led to minister in Gouverneur, New York, a larger town than the little communities of Jefferson County. Father Nash, a praying friend and companion of the revivalist, trekked over to Gouverneur to tell the church that Charles was on his way to preach to them.

Gouverneur lay some thirty miles distant from Jefferson County. It was a full day's journey in those times. As Finney set out, the heavens opened, sending a deluge of rain. The going proved most difficult, but perhaps it was a symbol of another kind of outpouring from heaven that Finney would soon see. The dark clouds that brought the deluge were also prophetic; ominous clouds of resistance threatened to roll across the preacher's sky.

The time for Finney's first meeting had already been set; the people expected him to preach the first night he arrived in town. The rain forced a late arrival, and at the church the people had given up, thinking the evangelist would not reach them that day. Father Nash stood, about to dismiss the congregation, when Finney burst in. Being quickly introduced, the evangelist announced a preaching service in an hour, saying he must have a little time for rest and recuperation after the drenching journey. When the set hour arrived, the folks packed the house. People shuffled up to the very edge of their seats in expectancy.

Finney had no time to prepare a formal message, but, as he said, "The Lord gave me a text." The Word took immediate and powerful effect, as it invariably does when preached in the power of the Holy Spirit. The people, deeply convicted, began to cry out to God. A revival was underway. But as soon as the Spirit of God began to move through the ministry of the Word, opposition reared its ugly head.

The first wave of resistance came through a noted physician, an avid and committed universalist. He challenged Finney to debate the issue. Charles, however, little relished a debate unless exact terms and methods could be agreed upon. He knew how aggressively "evangelistic" the universalists of his day could be. Nevertheless, he felt constrained to enter into dialogue with the universalistic doctor. So into the fray he flew. His quick lawyer's mind and argumentation (Finney was an ex-lawyer) soon put him in command of the situation. The debate seemed over before it began. The good doctor trudged home devastated. He could not remain still; he paced and paced about the house. His wife, a dedicated Christian, finally asked him, "What is the matter?" He looked at her and grunted, "Nothing." "Doctor, have you seen Mr. Finney this morning?" she asked. This brought the physician to a halt and he literally burst into tears. "Yes," he acknowledged, "and he has turned my weapons on my own head."

The outcome of that first wave of opposition turned out to be a great victory for Finney. In a very short time the doctor was soundly converted. Being an outspoken leader, his conversion profoundly touched the entire universalist camp in Gouverneur. One by one they turned to Christ until the revival gripped them all and ended their resistance to the awakening.

Satanic strategy did not stagnate, however. An evangelical church began opposing Finney. This deeply disturbed the evangelist. He must have felt much like Moses; God's own people standing in opposition to the work. The problem revolved around the mode of baptism. Being a Presbyterian, Finney did not stress baptism by immersion in his meetings. This upset the opposing evangelical group, who did practice that form of baptism. Finney was not at all resistant to baptism by immersion for those who wished it. As a matter of fact, he himself baptized by immersion about a dozen people in a previous meeting in Antwerp, New York. Finney and Nash, however, recognized the seriousness of the situation. They well knew the opposers were thoroughgoing evangelical Christians and that their resistance to the movement could become a real impediment to the entire work of God, even more serious than the universalists' threat. So Finney and Nash, his praying partner, gave themselves to fervent intercession.

One Sunday, a group of young men, under the opposition's influence, irreverently stalked into Finney's service, obviously intending to stir up trouble. Tension filled the air. As the service started and the meeting progressed, suddenly Father Nash stood up, struck the pew in front of him with his fist, and with eyes blazing at the young rebels cried out, "Now, mark you, young men! God will break your ranks in less than one week, either by converting some of you, or by sending some of you to hell. He will do this as certainly as the Lord is my God!" The house became still as death. Presumptuous? Finney at first thought so; he said he regretted Brother Nash had gone so far. But now the gauntlet had been thrown down.

Monday came. Nothing happened. On Tuesday, the leader of the young men sought out Finney, obviously in deep distress. As Charles spoke the words of salvation to the young agitator, the young man began to weep as a child. He gave his life to Christ. "What shall I do now, Mr. Finney?" he asked. The evangelist told the new convert to go immediately to all his friends, tell them what had happened, and urge them to receive God's forgiveness. He set out, and before the week drew to a close, nearly every young man was wonderfully won to the Lord. Father Nash had spoken in the Spirit after all.

God got the final victory. Resistance and irreverence from every quarter dried up. Soon the entire community found itself swept along in the mighty moving of God. So profound was the outpouring that, as Finney said, "The great majority of them [the Gouverneur community] were converted to Christ." Irreverence and opposition to God's work must be faced, rooted out, and broken. This was true for Moses' day and Finney's day; it is also true for ours.

Finally, in Israel's case, it becomes clear that the holiness of a reviving God forces into bold relief the last resort of rebellion: *idolatry and sensuality*. "Make us gods" (Exodus 32:1). Of course, the Jews did not wish to forsake religion, they just wanted to shed the moral demands of real religion. So religious materialism took over. Hear them: "Make us gods, Aaron, religion is good. Make us gods, Aaron, worship has social and psychological value. Make us gods, Aaron, religion gives a sense of security and makes you feel good. Make us gods, Aaron, we are religious creatures. Make us gods, Aaron."

And there will always be an "Aaron" to design the kind of gods we want. We may even call the religious exercise "Christianity." Remember, Aaron made the golden calf and called a feast to *Yahweh*. What a wicked combination: a golden calf and Yahweh! An abominable brand of syncretistic worship emerged wherein the people "sat down to eat and to drink, and rose up to play" (Exodus 32:6, KJV). "Rose up to play" means the people fell into sexual orgies. The same verb is employed in Genesis 26:8 when Isaac was discovered "fondling" his wife. That is how low Israel sank in the name of religion.

Syncretistic Religion

Israel slipped into syncretism at its worst. Whether Aaron attempted to combine the worship of Apis, the bull god of Egypt, or the Semitic Baalism worship of Canaan, with Yahweh worship; to mix *any* human-generated religion or philosophy with the true worship of God, as revealed in the Scriptures, is an abomination. The Jews, however, were skilled rationalizers; as long as Yahweh was somehow injected into the worship, they reasoned it would be acceptable. Poor Aaron did not see the peril of a syncretic idolatry or the tragedy of a sensual high as a substitute for the spiritual worship of a holy and jealous God. The Lord said to Moses: "I have seen this people, and behold, it is a stiff-necked people" (Exodus 32:9, RSV). Moving away from pure worship of the holy God is rebellion, no matter what we call it to justify the act. We must never forget the exclusive element in our Christian faith. Jesus said, "I am the way, and the truth, and the life; no one comes to the Father, but by me" (John 14:6, RSV). Peter reiterated the same truth when he preached: "There is salvation in no one else, for there is no other name under heaven given among men by which we must be saved" (Acts 4:12, RSV). Jesus Christ cannot be placed in the panoply of the gods and thus loose the biblical truth that He alone is God's way of salvation. The Scriptures speak with crystal clarity; no one finds God in redemption except through Jesus Christ alone. The modern-day spirit of syncretism and/or universalism violates all the Bible has to say concerning the Gospel of Christ. Yet, the syncretistic spirit is not a modern day phenomenon. As we have seen, Aaron tried it. But in his attempt to mix the bull-god Apis with the true and living God, he paid dearly. So will his twentieth-century counterparts.

We all recognize that this "exclusiveness" of the Gospel presents problems and raises questions about those who never hear the Word. Yet, the alternative to saying salvation rests in Jesus alone precipitates a much larger problem, for it undercuts the entire missionary-evangelistic ministry of the church, not to mention the violence it does to the Scriptures. Moreover, there has never been a revival where the exclusiveness of Christianity has not become prominent and thus filled believers with missionary, evangelistic zeal. As Michael Green, New Testament scholar, has aptly put it:

> Now if you believe that outside of Christ there is no hope, it is impossible to possess an atom of human love without being gripped by a great desire to bring men to this one way of salvation. We are not surprised, therefore, to find that concern for the state of the unevangelized was one of the great driving forces behind Christian preaching . . . in the early Church.[3]

Why do theologians, preachers, and people get off track on this issue? Not to sound ungracious or unloving, but it must be said that it is sin, not broadness of mind, which blinds one to God's truth concerning the need of Jesus Christ alone.

Oh, the tragedy of our iniquity! We seemingly forget so easily what our Puritan forefathers knew so well: "The exceeding sinfulness of sin." It blinds, bends, benights, and finally blasphemes God. God is utterly holy. He will not condone or excuse iniquity. Therefore, we must "turn from our wicked ways." Refusal to confront our sin stops revival in its tracks. There will never be a lasting revival of true religion until we deal with sin. If we will not "turn from our wicked ways," God may well say to us, as He said to Moses, "Let me alone, that my wrath may burn hot against them" (Exodus 32:10, RSV).

"Let me alone!" What a strange phrase! Was someone "bothering" God? Can anyone "upset" the Lord, so that He actually says, "Let me alone!" Could it be Moses was praying to the point he "irritated" God? Was prayer "hindering" the Lord? Is God bound by our prayers? Can one pray too much? What is happening? This leads to another vital truth in the revival account of the Exodus. Regardless of exactly what our Lord meant by the statement, "Let me alone!", one thing is certain, revival demands prayer.

The Holiness of God in Revival Demands Human Intercessors

In preparation for an evangelistic conference in California, the program director contracted for the theme of the conference to be painted on a large banner. It was to read "Heart Cry for Revival." When the director went to the painters to get the finished product, he saw that the artist had inadvertently painted, "Heart Cry for Survival." In principle it was not a mistake at all. Sin will inevitably slay any person, nation, or church. In the light of our contemporary, deep, and profound national and church needs, it is surely revival or perish. Right there, in the face of desperate need, intercession becomes the essential element. E. M. Bounds expressed it correctly:

> What the church needs today is not more machinery or better, not new organizations or more novel methods, but men whom the Holy Ghost can use—men of prayer, men mighty in prayer. The Holy Ghost does not flow through methods, but through men. He does not come on machinery, but on men. He does not anoint plans, but men—*men of prayer*.

If revival ever comes, it will be because someone prayed. This truth has been reiterated numerous times, but the point cannot be labored too much.

In September of 1794, a group of New England ministers grew deeply concerned over the spiritual situation of their day. They met at Lebanon, Connecticut, and after spending some time in prayer, agreed to unite their efforts to promote a "Concert of Prayer for Revival."* They issued a circular letter which set forth their objectives. This letter, signed by twenty-three ministers, was sent to all the pastors and churches of every Christian denomination in the United States. The letter contained the following proposal:

> In execution of this plan, it is proposed that the ministers and churches of every Christian denomination should be invited to maintain public prayer and praise, accompanied with such instructions from God's Word as might be judged proper, on every first Tuesday of the four quarters of the year, beginning with the first Tuesday of January 1795, at two o'clock in the afternoon, if the plan of concert should then be ripe for a beginning, and so continuing from quarter to quarter and from year to year, until the good providence of God prospering our endeavors, we shall obtain the blessing for which we pray.[4]

The proposed ministry of prayer met with general approval by many individuals, churches, and several denominational bodies. Initial reports concerning the Concert of Prayer indicated that its impact was quite widespread and influential. God was apparently about to do something great. The fervent prayer continued for two years. Suddenly revival began to break out here and there, first in New England. The early phase of America's Second Great Awakening had begun and soon the revival spirit spread over the land. Only heaven can recount all that took place in those glorious days. In some senses it even exceeded in power America's First Great Awakening.

Moses, in the moment of Israel's deep sin and need, realized to the fullest extent the principle of prayer. If God's grace is to be experienced, intercession becomes imperative. And Israel needed God's grace desperately. Their only hope after their heinous rebellion was the sheer mercy of God. So we see Moses, on his face before God, pleading for grace. As a man of prayer, Moses did not fail his people. The Bible says:

> Moses besought the LORD his God, and said, "O LORD, why does thy wrath burn hot against thy people, whom thou hast brought forth out of the land of Egypt with great power

---

*The "Concert of Prayer" was the method promoted by Jonathan Edwards in America's First Great Awakening.

and with a mighty hand? Why should the Egyptians say, 'With evil intent did he bring them forth, to slay them in the mountains, and to consume them from the face of the earth?' Turn from thy fierce wrath, and repent of this evil against thy people. Remember Abraham, Isaac, and Israel, thy servants, to whom thou didst swear by thine own self, and didst say to them, 'I will multiply your descendants as the stars of heaven, and all this land that I have promised I will give to your descendants, and they shall inherit it for ever'" (Exodus 32:11–13, RSV).

God said, "Let me alone." But Moses would not cease from interceding. The emergency Israel faced was so great, he had to pray—pray as never before—and at all costs. Of course God honored it, and was actually in it all. One commentator beautifully expressed the extremity of the situation: "In the emergency which had arisen, everything depended on the mediator, and in His grace God had provided one who would stand in the breach."[5] The Israelites desperately needed intercession; the Bible says they were running wild, casting off all resistance (Exodus 32:25). The same verb is used in Proverbs 29:18: "Where there is no prophecy the people cast off restraint" (Proverbs 29:18, RSV). So Moses interceded regardless of all circumstances. When those conditions infect a people, the spiritually sensitive must go to their knees as did Moses. Three principles permeated Moses' prevailing prayers for mercy and restoration.

Moses' Prayer

1. *Moses reminded God that the people are the Lord's redeemed.* Free, sovereign grace had made them God's people. Only that depth of grace will keep them such. So Moses prayed for *more* grace: "But Moses besought the LORD his God, and said, 'O LORD, why does thy wrath burn hot against thy people, whom thou has brought forth out of the Land of Egypt with great power and with a mighty hand?'" (Exodus 32:11, RSV). Even if they are "a stiff-necked people" (Exodus 32:9), they are still God's people. "Grant grace," Moses pleaded. The basic principle of revival already seen surfaces again; namely, God first showers His grace on His own covenant people. God cannot revive that which never had life. He revives only that which at

one time possessed life. Simply put, the revival begins with God's people, thus we pray, "Wilt thou not revive *us* again, that *thy people* may rejoice in thee?" (Psalm 85:6, RSV).

2. *Moses further reminded God that His reputation was at stake.* "Why should the Egyptians say," Moses cried, " 'With evil intent did he bring them forth' " (Exodus 32:12, RSV). Moses was right in some sense; God puts His name on the line with His people. If believers are not graciously revived in holiness, how will the world know He is holy? If we do not turn from our wicked ways, what will the lost think of our God?

3. *Moses called before God the fact that Yahweh is known for His faithfulness and grace toward His covenant people:* "Remember Abraham, Isaac, and Israel, thy servants, to whom thou didst swear by thine own self" (Exodus 32:13, RSV). "God," pleads Moses, "they did not deserve to be brought into thy covenant, you brought them in through grace. Oh, God, once more have mercy on your people. Be faithful to your covenant, Oh, holy God, turn them from their wicked ways."

Moses pleaded with such passion that finally he cried out: "Alas, this people have sinned a great sin; they have made for themselves gods of gold. But now, if thou wilt forgive their sin—and if not, blot me, I pray thee, out of thy book which thou hast written" (Exodus 32:31–32, RSV). What a spirit of sacrifice and love for a people—a people in sin, no less! Paul displayed a similar spirit when he said, "I am speaking the truth in Christ, I am not lying; my conscience bears me witness in the Holy Spirit, that I have great sorrow and unceasing anguish in my heart. For I could wish that I myself were accursed and cut off from Christ for the sake of my brethren, my kinsmen by race" (Romans 9:1–3, RSV). That's praying! That agonizing intercession on behalf of others is the depth of burden that moves God to action, and that in turn changes the course of history. After Moses prayed, the Bible says, "And the LORD repented of the evil which he thought to do to his people" (Exodus 32:14, RSV). Moses would not leave God alone, and God honored it. Actually, it is probably proper to say God did *not* want Moses to "leave Him alone." Judgment was averted. God, the omnipotent God, in grace moves on wings of the fervent cry of His servants. How marvelous shines forth the mercy and grace of our holy God. When His faithful pray, He revives His people. It was certainly

118

true for Israel. As Walter C. Kaiser has pointed out so well, "There are few places in the Bible where such a wonderful expression of God's compassion and full forgiveness can be found simultaneously."[6] The power of prayer touches the heart of God and unleashes marvelous results.

We need not be reminded of the gods of gold our people have made for themselves. But where are the prevailing "Moseses," those willing to die unless revival comes? Occasionally they are found. It happened in the Hebrides some years ago.

In 1949, on the Island of Lewis in the Hebrides, those rather bleak, windswept isles off the northwest coast of Scotland, a little handful of "Moseses" were so burdened for an awakening on their island that they were meeting for prayer two or three nights a week in an old barn outside their village. Night after night they pleaded with God for revival. Their burden grew until it became almost unbearable. Often they prayed into the morning hours.

This went on for days, weeks, and months. Yet, the heavens seemed as brass. One night, one of the younger men stood up and said in typical British idiom, "Men, this is so much rubbish. Could it be that we, the very ones most concerned for a spiritual awakening, are the very ones standing in its way? God has laid on my heart a verse of Scripture. The psalmist said, "Who shall ascend the hill of the LORD? And who shall stand in his holy place? He who has clean hands and a pure heart" (Psalm 24:3, RSV). With that word, God suddenly opened heaven upon them and revealed himself in consuming holiness. They were literally smitten to the floor of the barn, cut to heart with conviction. They saw their unclean hands and impure hearts as never before. They poured out their broken confession. It was an "Isaiah experience" repeated; the holy God had confronted them and they cried out, "Woe to me . . . I am ruined!" (Isaiah 6:1–5). Then, just as suddenly, the glory and joy of the Lord swept over them like a surging torrent. They must have had glowing faces as did Moses!

After composing themselves, it was now early in the morning, they made their way back to their homes, but to their amazement they found virtually everyone in the village up and gathered at the police station. On inquiring, they discovered that at the very hour the convicting Holy Spirit had prostrated them in the barn, the same Spirit of conviction had fallen on practically everyone in town, awakening them from sleep and deeply convicting each one of their lostness. Unable to sleep because of the deep conviction, they dressed, gathered at the police station trying to find out how to be saved. The faithful few had prevailed before God, as did Moses for apostate Israel. Remember, "the prayer of a righteous man has great power in its effects" (James 5:16, RSV). Before dawn broke that day, many in the town experienced the light of Christ dawning in their souls.

We find such moments almost incredulous. But that is because most of us have never seen a sweeping spiritual awakening. And if any human reason can be found why we have not seen a profound revival in our day, it is because we have not permitted the holiness of God to drive us to our knees, turn us from our wicked ways, and make us intercessors like Moses. Above all, God is Holy; we must turn from our wicked ways—our wicked prayerlessness.

Finally, Moses' awakening experience teaches us to search out our goals in Christ's service.

The Holiness of God in Revival Determines Human Intentions

In the end, we must decide what we really want in our Christian lives and service, what our intentions truly are. That demands facing several central issues.

First of all, if we mean business with God, we cannot condone any compromise with evil. No neutral ground can be found; it is either God or the devil. No rationalization! No excuses! Look how poor Aaron tried: "I said to them [the people], 'Let any who have gold take it off'; so they gave it to me, and I threw it into the fire, and there came out this calf" (Exodus 32:24, RSV). Did Aaron actually expect Moses to believe that? What an excuse; expecting his brother to accept such a ridiculous miracle story. "Aaron," Moses must have said, "at least be honest!" God never honors lies. Perhaps the worse brand of falsehood is to lie to ourselves about our religious experiences—or lack of them. The essential difference between Moses and Aaron centered in the fact that Moses had been on Mount Sinai listening to God while Aaron had been in the valley listening to the people. Those who do not practice the presence of God will inevitably end up in trouble. And if one is a leader, others will follow his example. Aaron tragically led the people into sin; at least he did not restrain them.

Secondly, we cannot sidestep sheer, uncompromising *obedience*. Moses cried out: "Who is on the LORD's side?" (Exodus 32:26). That cry always constitutes the foundational question. Remember Samuel's smarting statement to half-obedient, half-rebellious King Saul: "Behold, to obey is better than sacrifice, and to hearken than the fat of rams" (1 Samuel 15:22, RSV).

It all reduces itself to this: We cannot avoid repentance in the light of an encounter with the holy God. The pungent term "repentance" means to change; to change our minds, our attitudes, our entire direction of life. Repentance constitutes a total turning to God and an abandonment of all evil and an absolute surrender to the lordship of Christ in one's life. We simply must "turn from our wicked ways." It is either repentance or judgment. In Israel "that day about three thousand of the people died" (Exodus 32:28). Sin in God's people is that serious. Any hope for revival forces this fact to the fore: Repentance is vital. God is holy, and that holiness demands the same in His people through deep repentance and faith.

Nonetheless, the Mount Sinai story ends with a beautiful epilogue. When God revealed His holiness, the Israelites genuinely repented. They "turned from their wicked ways," as our theme text demands. The Bible says, "Therefore the people of Israel stripped themselves of their ornaments, from Mt. Horeb onward" (Exodus 33:6, RSV). They had taken off their jewelry earlier to make an idolatrous calf, and it almost killed them. Now they stripped it off in repentance to God, and they found life. Entering a deep experience of repentance, they were mightily revived. They learned what Isaiah learned: "For thus saith the high and lofty One that inhabiteth eternity, whose name is Holy; I dwell in the high and holy place, with him also that is of a contrite and humble spirit, to revive the spirit of the humble, and to revive the heart of the contrite ones" (Isaiah 57:15, KJV).

Conclusion

Peter posed the proper question: "Since all these things are thus to be dissolved, what sort of persons ought you to be in lives of holiness and godliness?" (2 Peter 3:11, RSV). There stands the issue! Our hymnologists were perhaps more insightful than many realize; they placed as hymn number one in most of our songbooks:

Holy, holy, holy! Lord God Almighty!
All thy works shall praise thy name,
In earth, and sky, and sea;
Holy, holy, holy; merciful and mighty!
God in three Persons, blessed Trinity!

From the awesome glow of Sinai, Israel, now awakened, cleansed, renewed, and revived, went on to inherit the Promised Land. May we join them in that joyous, holy, revival journey.

Not Me, Lord!

In a Spiritual Awakening God Reveals Himself as

GRACE

Therefore, Experience "Forgiveness of Sins."

JONAH 1–4

Introduction

History is filled with the fact that at times God in His providence does the very thing we would least expect. On occasion He will even use seemingly bizarre methods, not to mention unusual people. Refreshing revival seasons often unfold in that setting. Of course, God himself is not in any sense of the word bizarre, nor does He ever act in a capricious, arbitrary manner. All that can be said is simply that His ways are on occasion inscrutable—"past finding out." We must beware of making the presumptuous mistake of the brash, not-too-literate preacher who one Sunday morning during the worship hour read a cryptic passage of Scripture, took off his spectacles, closed the Bible with a bang and said, "Brothers and sisters, this morning I intend to explain the unexplainable, find out the undefinable, ponder over the imponderable, and unscrew the inscrutable." God's ways are often inscrutable, going quite beyond our ability to grasp all their fullness, and we must studiously avoid presumption and arrogance, thinking we can explain all His actions.

If any rationalization can be found for God's unusual acts in reviving grace, the clue is usually discovered in the fact that traditionalism—business as usual—will rarely precipitate a profound moving of the Spirit. As the poet put it:

All our fathers have been churchmen,
Nineteen hundred years or so.
And to every new suggestion
They always answered, "NO!"

When such an attitude actually exists, the rich soil is depleted; therefore, the harvest will be meager. May it never be written on our spiritual tombstones what is engraved on the cemetery monument to the British soldiers killed at Lexington and Concord during the American Revolution: "These came 3,000 miles to keep the past upon the throne." When such a spirit prevails in the church, an awakening is sorely needed.

So God in grace, with the goal of reviving His apathetic people, performs the startling, the unusual, even at times the apparently bizarre. Therefore, when those awakening moments arrive, even if we fail to understand it all, we will be wise to ascribe it to His ultimate wisdom and, above all, to His free, reviving, revealed *grace*. Revival invariably blossoms as a result of God's fathomless *grace*, inscrutable as it may be. Moreover, the grace of God invariably moves people to repentance and forgiveness. And because His reviving grace abounds to all, all can experience the "forgiveness of our sins."

The Shantung Revival

This prime principle of awakening grace and the subsequent forgiveness of sins are perfectly illustrated in one of God's unfathomable works in Shantung Province, Northeast China, in 1927. This great awakening, referred to in chapter one, had its birth in turmoil. The Baptist missionaries, along with those of other groups, were under pressure from the deep unrest caused by the marching armies of Sun Yat-sen led by Marshall Chaeng Kai-Shek. A pitched battle with the old feudal warlords raged in full fury. When the so-called "Rape of Nanking" took place, an alarmed American government called the twenty-four Baptist missionaries from Shantung to the seaport city of Chefoo. They congregated in a very small mission compound with only two houses. There God accomplished one of His unusual acts of grace.

It all started quite simply. The missionaries decided they should pray together for an hour each morning. Concerned for the Chinese believers they had left on the field, they desperately wanted them to stand true to Christ during the upheaval. They were also concerned for their own well-being. So they started to intercede, believing our theme text that those who "seek his face and pray" will surely experience God's grace. God honored their prayer commitment with His gracious presence. The first day they prayed for an hour, the second day for two hours. Soon they were praying till noon, not so much for the Chinese believers, but for themselves. The burden for an awakening among their own group soon all but overwhelmed them.

Then Miss Marie Monson, an evangelical Lutheran missionary from Norway, joined the prayer band and began to share what God had done in her life. Through the challenge of Miss Monson, along with fervent prayer, the firstfruits of revival burst forth. It proved to be the early harbinger of a general awakening.

After the political crisis subsided, the missionaries journeyed back to their fields. As soon as they arrived at their stations, a refreshing revival deluge rained down everywhere. A new day for China arrived. The work received God's awakening touch.

Venerable Shantung missionary Dr. W. B. Glass, after his retirement, would come to my small student pastorate in Ft. Worth, Texas. He would share with our congregation the glories of those revival days. We thrilled to hear him tell how the Chinese churches of Shantung filled as converts came to Christ by the hundreds and thousands. The Shantung seminary, where Dr. Glass had served as a professor during the revival, overflowed with new students. Before the awakening there had been only two men preparing for the ministry, now the seminary was full to overflowing. The revival broadened and deepened until the entire nation finally felt the impact of the awakening. Dr. Glass helped stoke the fire for revival in my heart and put a prayer in all of us for God to do once again what He had done for those missionaries in 1927. Surely we all cry out for a fresh awakening! And we must be willing to let God be God and do it His way with whom He pleases, whether we understand it or not.

And there are times, in fact, when God in His own sovereign way initiates a revival in the face of even reluctant servants, as we see in the case of Jonah.

Jonah, that reluctant, rebellious, retreating Old Testament prophet, apparently did not feel or even seek much of a Spirit-inspired movement. Nonetheless, a work of God's grace was planned for that man.

The Revival Under Jonah

As the book of Jonah opens, we find the prophet of God resting in Jerusalem quite content with the spiritual status quo. He apparently enjoyed "business as usual." Then, right in the midst of his comfort and ease, God did one of His unusual things; He said to the prophet, "Go to Nineveh, Jonah, I want to revive that great city. I desire to shed my free grace on them. They deserve it not, but I want to forgive their sin." Jonah almost reeled under the shock of such a summons. Although God's ways are inscrutable, surely He could not mean Nineveh to experience His grace. Jonah must have replied something like this: "Go to Nineveh? That wicked city? Not me, LORD! They are Gentiles! Not me, LORD! All they deserve is judgment, not grace. Not me, LORD." He failed to grasp God as a God of grace who delights to revive "wicked cities," and use strange instruments in the process. That was unbelievable to Jonah's Jewish mind-set. His lack of understanding, combined with not a little rebellion, caused the reluctant prophet to take ship immediately—and that in the opposite direction. Nineveh lay east, but Jonah boarded a ship and went west toward Tarshish in Spain. It can hardly go unnoticed that invariably "a ship going to Tarshish" (Jonah 1:2) waits for those who attempt to escape God's will. Be assured, Satan will always provide passage on a "ship" to forsake God's will. But the trip is always futile. You cannot hide from God. The psalmist learned that lesson:

> If I make my bed in Sheol, thou art there! If I take the wings of the morning and dwell in the uttermost parts of the sea, even there thy hand shall lead me, and thy right hand shall hold me. If I say, "Let only darkness cover me, and the light about me be night," even the darkness is not dark to thee, the night is bright as the day; for darkness is as light with thee (Psalm 139:8–12, RSV).

Jonah should have known that; for he himself confessed that the Lord was "God of heaven, who made the sea and dry land"

(Jonah 1:9, RSV). If He made Jerusalem, He surely made Tarshish. No one can escape from God. But so clouded and confused by rebellion was the fleeing prophet, he could not even keep his basic theology straight.

But the penetrating question is: Why would God use a rebellious prophet like Jonah for a gracious revival ministry? Jonah was just like the two characters in Bunyan's *Pilgrim's Progress*, named Timorous and Mistrust, who confused and baffled Pilgrim. When Pilgrim met them, he asked, "Sirs, what's the matter? You run the wrong way." Imagine, God's own servants running the wrong way. Such was Jonah. Yet, God called to revival this "wrong way" prophet, as strange and inscrutable as it seems. But that points up a very important revival reality. God often selects in grace those whom we, in our limited human wisdom, would never choose.

God in Revival Grace Often Calls the Most Unlikely Characters

Look at this prophet called Jonah. The narrative reads:

> Now the word of the LORD came unto Jonah the son of Amittai, saying, "Arise, go to Nineveh, that great city, and cry against it; for their wickedness is come up before me." But Jonah rose to flee to Tarshish from the presence of the LORD. He went down to Joppa and found a ship going to Tarshish: so he paid the fare, and went on board, to go with them to Tarshish, away from the presence of the LORD (Jonah 1:1–3, RSV).

Jonah proved to be a particularly paradoxical prophet. To begin with, he hailed from Gath-hepha in Galilee, a city that belonged to the tribe of Zebulum (2 Kings 14:25). It was a remote, rather obscure part of Israel. Could anything significant come out of that isolated region? But as already stressed, God often raises up unusual personalities from unusual places to fulfill His unusual plans. Jonah preached during the reign of Jeroboam. He had prophesied Jeroboam would restore the coast of Israel, and it came to pass. Jonah had been used by God, but it seems some sort of apathy and unconcern had invaded his spiritual life. Here is where the paradox of God choosing such a man really begins. The Bible tells us four things, four rather sad things, about the prophet chosen by God for what could be his greatest hour of ministry.

First of all, as already implied, Jonah's life smacked of a basic *rebellion*. He knew God, yet acted at times as if he did not, at least concerning Nineveh. He loved God, but not quite fully. He served God, and yet not completely. A streak of stubbornness lurked in his secret soul that when the crucial crunch came, he just could not do what truly mattered. Some love, some service, some surrender, but not what really matters: *absolute surrender*. True, his contemporary culture was hardly conducive to commitment. He lived in the Northern Kingdom under King Jeroboam II—a rebellious time indeed. King and people approached life as if God were dead. But that constituted no excuse for God's prophet. The Lord lives and demands obedience regardless of one's surroundings. The tragedy of rebellion centers in this: no obedience, no revival.

Jonah probably harbored some *bigotry*. One can almost hear the prophet justifying himself for his reluctance: "After all, I am a Jew. The Jews have no dealings with the Ninevites. The chosen race is my heritage. Jews can boast being the exclusive elect of God. We cannot touch unclean things—or people." Many of the Jews felt so selfishly superior in religion and culture, they held in horror the mere thought of any fellowship with anyone else, let alone "heathen" Ninevites. That's bigotry. The terrible tragedy of such an exclusivism centers in the fact that Jonah and the Jews failed to understand that God never profoundly revives His own people without touching all people and reaching every segment of society. Cultural snobbery or narrow denominationalism has no place in a true spiritual awakening. Actually, God's condemnation of Jonah's rebellious bigotry forms the main message of the book. If the Scriptures say anything, they declare God's love and grace to *all* people. His matchless mercy reaches out to everyone.

Jonah was not only prejudiced, he was *unconcerned*. He completely missed the point that should always characterize God's true servants. Paul expressed the proper approach in his epistle to the Romans:

I am under obligation both to Greeks and to barbarians, both to the wise and to the foolish: so I am eager to preach the gospel to you also who are in Rome. For I am not ashamed of the gospel: it is the power of God for salvation to every one who has faith, to the Jew first *and also to the Greek*. For in it the righteousness of God is revealed through faith for faith; as it is written, "He who through faith is righteous shall live" (Romans 1:14–17, RSV).

Jonah utterly failed to see in his myopic vision the plight of the poor Ninevites. Such spiritual shortsightedness always grows out of a failure to grasp God's all-inclusive love. That, in turn, will force one to miss God's redemptive plan for all people.* God intensely intends His people to go tell all the lost about Jesus Christ and His power to save, *wherever* they can be found. Unbelievers all over the world stumble along in darkness and sin until they hear and receive the Gospel. Christians must evangelize them. Someone once asked Charles H. Spurgeon, "Do you really believe those who have never heard the Gospel are lost?" Spurgeon retorted, "Do you really believe those who say they believe the Gospel and never share it are saved?" One of the root issues with Jonah, and his like-minded spiritual kin, was mere unconcern. People without Jesus Christ are lost, and Christians should be deeply burdened. No true believer should attempt to sidestep that concern on dubious theological or practical grounds. Jonah's problem was that he was all wrapped up in his own interests—and those interests may even have been his "ministry." Simply put, he forgot how desperately people need the Lord. When will we realize, people *need* the Lord? But when God's people do become burdened and concerned, great things in renewal can happen. It has happened before.

The Lennox Awakening

At the close of the eighteenth century, the general apathy over spiritual matters and disregard for God's Word began to breed deep anxiety among the faithful, spiritual-minded church

---

*This is not to imply theological universalism. People must hear the Gospel and repent and believe in Jesus Christ as the only Savior if they are to be saved.

members at Lennox, Massachusetts. They well knew that any community that ignores God's truth and develops a negligent attitude toward spiritual matters will soon see decay settling in and the eroding away of their society. So, they begged their pastor to schedule some special meetings for Bible study and prayer, looking for an outpouring of the Holy Spirit. The pastor, fortunately, had spiritual discernment to approve such meetings. That boded for better days. At one of the early meetings, the divine authority of the Scripture became the subject of discussion. The people came to realize that the Holy Bible stands as the very voice of God to a guilty world. Suddenly the solemn truth and power of the Word of God gripped the people; the lost who were present actually trembled at the prospect of what the Bible says about judgment and eternity. Christians themselves grew more fervent in prayer. Then the revival broke. The awakening that followed became a renewal of the authority, power, and demands of God's Word. Rev. Samuel Shepherd put it this way:

> When God is about to bestow spiritual blessings upon a people, it is His usual method first to awaken His professed friends out of sleep. Before a single instance of conviction was known in this place, in the Spring of the year 1799, many of the members of this church, in the course of a few days, manifested anxious concern for the cause of Christ. A spirit of prayer and supplication seemed to be given them and as soon as Zion travailed, she brought forth children.[1]

The power of God fell, the believers were revived, the saving Gospel was preached, and the rebellious were regenerated.

But Jonah, seemingly fearful to launch out on God's clear word, refused to undertake the Nineveh venture. The fourth characteristic that typified the rebellious, bigoted, unconcerned "man of God" (if one dare call him that) lies in the fact that he may well have been plain *scared.* That seems a safe conjecture in the context of the entire scenario. It is somewhat understandable, however. Nineveh must have overwhelmed him. Nineveh boasted itself as a great and powerful city. Furthermore, Jonah was probably a relatively old man at the time of the call of God. But the Lord does not rely on the mere strength of youth, and no "Nineveh" can be a match for God's power. Jonah failed to realize "God has not given us the spirit of fear but of love, power, and a sound mind" (2 Timothy 1:7, RSV).

Of course, Jonah was not totally without regard for God. That would be too harsh a judgment; he just failed to be filled with God's Spirit, and hence lacked the grace to face the Ninevites. Yet, *God chose him* for the mission. Again the question comes to the fore: Why did God ever choose such a rebellious, bigoted, unconcerned, fearful man for such a Herculean task? Amos was a contemporary of Jonah; why didn't the Lord choose him, or Hosea, another contemporary prophet? Why Jonah? In revival, our Lord often seems to choose those who need His grace most, even a Jonah. But it takes a deep experience of grace to declare that grace to others. Here shines forth the beautiful point of it all: The grace of God is sufficient to fulfill His will even if we have a thousand weaknesses and sins. Remember, God uses any of us in spite of ourselves. In revival grace God has promised: *He will strengthen us and forgive our sins.* He did it for Jonah; He can do it for us. That leads to another quite fascinating twist to the Jonah story.

God in Revival Grace Gives a Most Unlikely Commission

God certainly called the wayward prophet to preach in an exceedingly difficult place. "Go to Nineveh," the Lord had said. To Jonah it appeared as a most unlikely commission. Nineveh was a "great city," as the Bible declares (Jonah 1:2). Being the leading metropolis of the Assyrian empire, it had grown into the largest city in the world by Jonah's day. Sennacherib had fashioned it into the chief center of his empire. He built stately palaces and increased its fortifications. The Bible tells us in Jonah 3:3 it took three days just to walk around it. It rested on the east bank of the Tigris River, 250 miles north of Babylon. Archaeologists have calculated that the metropolitan area occupied the entire confluence of the Tigris and Upper Zab Rivers. It boasted as many as one million inhabitants. That is how Jonah would have viewed this "great city."*

But great Nineveh had also become a "wicked city" (Jonah 1:2). No doubt that made it most difficult for fearful Jonah. Pagan tradition held that the city was founded by the pagan god "Nim," whom they worshiped. Further, the temples of the Babylonian god Ishtar had been built by Manishtusu of the Dynasty of Akkad (c. 2425–2245 B.C.). Of course, Nineveh of Assyria may not have been any more morally or religiously corrupt than other cities, but idolatry—worshiping any god but Yahweh—stands in the sight of the true God as exceedingly wicked.

Moreover, Nineveh's godlessness gave it an image throughout the Middle East as a violent city. Jonah 3:8 speaks about the "violence which is in their hands." The prophet Nahum called Nineveh "that bloody city" (Nahum 3:1). The ruins archaeologists have uncovered dramatize that fact. The recovered freezes of the unearthed buildings reveal the cruelty of the Assyrians. They would cut off the hands, feet, ears, noses, and put out the eyes of their captured enemies. Little wonder Jonah trembled. They had pillaged and pitilessly ravaged the nations of the Mediterranean world. In reality, the traditional Assyrian god "Nim" had nothing to do with the founding of the city; Genesis 10:11 tells us Nimrod, a "mighty hunter," established the early community. That occurred in 2350 B.C. So they deified Nimrod and his bloody bow. Bloodshed was probably characteristic of their mind-set from the beginning. One could well imagine, therefore, the disdain they would have demonstrated toward anyone coming from little, insignificant Israel, denouncing their gods and proclaiming the wrath of Yahweh. Still, God said: "Go, Jonah, right in all that wicked, pagan violence. *Go right there!*" What an unlikely commission! What hope of any success in such a spot!

---

*Four towns are recorded in Genesis 10:11–12, as composing "that great city." Rehoboth-Ir, Caleh, Peson, and Calah. These and several other communities constituted the metropolitan area. Diodorous Seculus in the first century B.C. stated that Ninevah formated a quadrangle measuring 150 stadia by 90, 480 in circumference, or 60 miles. It was a three-day journey around it (Jonah 3:3).

The Message

Not only that, God declared, "I send you to that wicked, violent city to *proclaim judgment.*" How would the proud Ninevites ever tolerate such a message? No doubt it would cost Jonah his life, at least Jonah must have so reckoned. How much easier and safer, perhaps even reasonably enjoyable, it would have been for Jonah to condemn the sin and debauchery of Nineveh in his own circle in Israel. The prophet could well have cried in the security of his own tight-knit group, "Oh, God will judge that great, wicked city Nineveh, and make it as Sodom and Gomorrah. That's what they deserve, and that's what they will get. God will surely destroy those vile heathens." But that sort of attitude misses what God wishes to do. Jonah's group probably never sang:

> Marvelous grace of our loving Lord,
> Grace that exceeds our sin and our guilt!

But God shook Jonah to his very soul: "Jonah, leave your security and go to Nineveh and tell them boldly I'm about to fulfill your prophecies and vindicate your righteous indignation proclamations."

The Mission

This God we serve so often turns the tables on our self-righteous bigotry and calls us with a most unlikely commission. We dare not forget, God reveals himself as all grace and He deeply desires to forgive sins—even the sins of great, wicked, violent cities. As Jonah's experience in the big fish stands as something of a preview picture of the death and resurrection of Jesus (Matthew 12:39–41); the call to salvation, therefore, stands at the very core in the book of Jonah. Jonah's commission was, in the Old Testament sense, an "evangelistic" mission. Granted, the Ninevites were Israel's bitter foes; but our enemies, at least as we may view them, are not necessarily God's enemies. God wants to save them by His grace. Many centuries after Jonah, in England, the grace of God once again was freely bestowed on a wicked city. When that epitome of Puritan-pietism, Richard Baxter, came to the Anglican pastorate of Kiddeminster in the North of England, it likewise had degenerated into a wicked, violent, seventeenth-century community. But that godly pastor was "violent" too, as his Lord promised he could be. He determined to take the kingdom with "violence" (Matthew 11:12). He prayed, preached, witnessed, ministered, and agonized. He himself said, "I preach as a dying man to dying men." Finally, God in reviving grace moved into the midst of the sinfully sad situation, and the people suddenly came alive to Jesus Christ. Conversions abounded, sin was forgiven and forsaken, godliness flourished, and the power of the Spirit flowed in a reviving outpouring of God's unmerited favor. The entire city experienced a spiritual revolution. Scarcely a home in the entire parish failed to house a new convert. Our Lord truly does want to bestow grace and forgive sins. And what the God of grace did for Kiddeminster through Baxter, He can well do again. It all points out the next significant awakening principle.

God in Revival Grace Displays Most Unlikely Compassion

The gracious compassion of God exemplifies itself beautifully in the Jonah story. Our Lord's first act of loving grace centers in Jonah himself. As seen, Jonah fled from God: "Jonah rose up to flee to Tarshish from the presence of the LORD" (Jonah 1:3, RSV). But he paid dearly for it. Judgment came. It always does.

The story is well known: the fearful fleeing to Tarshish, the surging storm, the terror of the sailors, Jonah asleep in the hold of the ship. "What do you mean, you sleeper?" cried the captain. "Get up and call on your God" (Jonah 1:6). The pagan captain should be commended; he had more concern at that stage than did God's own prophet. Did Jonah pray? No! "Throw me overboard," pleaded the prophet. Eliminate the sleeper and you eliminate the storm. Jonah was so stubborn he would rather die than repent and go to Nineveh. So over the rail and into the sea he sank. And, "the LORD appointed a great fish to swallow up Jonah; and Jonah was in the belly of the fish three days and three nights" (Jonah 1:17, RSV).

Death, judgment, retribution, the end! The decree of God is just. That ends that saga. The prophet has perished. He's gone.

Or is he? Suddenly, we see Jonah not in heaven as one might expect, but of all places, in the fish's belly—*and still alive.*

The word "judgment" does not exhaust God's vocabulary; grace and forgiveness also stand out in bold relief in the divine dictionary. Actually, Jonah experienced God's "judging grace": judgment, but still grace. That is what put Jonah in the belly of the great fish.

It should be said at this point that some readers of the Jonah saga get too preoccupied with questions concerning the scientific possibility of a great fish swallowing a man and the man coming out alive. That is not the central issue of the story.* We should focus on the great God of grace who loves even the Ninevites and calls His people, even His wayward people, to preach repentance to them. Therefore, right in the belly of the fish, one of the most marvelous truths of the entire book shines forth. Right there Jonah discovered God's primary paradox of grace: Life comes out of death. No death, no life. This is why the story portrays such a graphic picture of the death and resurrection of our Lord Jesus Christ. Life out of death is one of God's inscrutable revival ways.

In the belly of the great fish, in that "judgment-grace" situation, Jonah did two very wise things. First, Jonah prayed to the Lord his God: "In my distress I called to the LORD" (Jonah 2:2). In essence he said, "Lord, I have made a tragic mistake; forgive my sin, I look to you." At last he learned to pray. Charles H. Spurgeon once said, "I had rather teach one man to pray than ten men to preach." Secondly, the prophet cried, "I with the voice of thanksgiving will sacrifice to thee . . . Deliverance belongs to the LORD!" (Jonah 2:9, RSV). When we not only pray, but *praise God* in faith for a deliverance we have not yet experienced in the "belly" of our

---

*Strangely, there have been recent, verifiable accounts of finding an entire human body in the stomach of certain whales. But that in itself does not verify the historicity of the Jonah story. It stands as true because it is God's Word. Moreover, our Lord Jesus Christ made reference to the account. That, it seems, should settle the historicity of the story.

"fish," then victory will certainly come. Billy Bray, the happy Welsh revivalist one time said, "Well friends, I have been taking vinegar and honey, but, praise the Lord, I've had the vinegar with a *spoon*, and the honey with a *ladle*." That spirit cannot be defeated. Joy constitutes a definite part of revival. One can almost hear Jonah inside the fish singing and praising God for His grace. No denizen of the deep could stand that. We read, "The LORD spoke to the fish, and it vomited out Jonah upon the dry land" (Jonah 2:10, RSV).

Then one of the most beautiful verses in all the Bible emerges. What marvelous grace it expresses: "Then the word of the LORD came to Jonah *a second time*" (Jonah 3:1). This great God who reveals himself as grace in revival *gives a second chance*. That is what the grace of God is all about. He will surely "forgive our sins" and let us try again. Jesus Christ creates a land of beginning again. Moreover, Jonah's personal revival led to a national revival. So often a spiritual awakening unfolds in that fashion; one person is revived and it suddenly becomes exceedingly contagious.

So off to Nineveh the recommissioned prophet ran, this time post-haste, chastised, cleansed, and recommissioned. Jonah's experience can be summed up in three simple points: (1) He ran *from* God, (2) He ran *into* God, (3) He ran *for* God. What did Jonah find when he arrived at that "great city." There another marvelous act of God's grace in revival reveals itself. The prophet must have been dumbstruck, for little did he realize what unusual consequences the free grace of God can bring about.

God in Revival Grace Demonstrates the Most Unlikely Consequences

A vital principle of revival emerges right at this point. When God's people get rightly revived, the Holy Spirit can begin to spread His grace-work abroad. A revival simply *must* impact the lives of the lost if it is to be called a true awakening. As pointed out, a true spiritual awakening becomes exceedingly contagious; it always spreads to the languishing lost. Furthermore, in that dynamic salvation work, the Spirit of God never moves in a vacuum; God uses His own revived people as His instrument to spread the work. A revival in the church invariably finds its culmination in the awakening of the whole community. But the initial work always takes place in individual believers' lives, Jonah being a perfect parable of the principle. Actually, the Nineveh revival began its work among unbelievers while Jonah was still at sea when the pagan sailors on the ship bound for Tarshish saw the dramatic demonstration of God's power. The Bible says, "The men feared the LORD exceedingly, and offered a sacrifice unto the LORD, and made vows" (Jonah 1:16, KJV). God in grace can even use our rebellion, but so much more our obedience. Let's observe Nineveh's response now that the prophet found himself in God's will.

Nineveh's Response

Would anyone have ever believed that Nineveh would actually accept the preaching of a reluctant yet repentant prophet of Israel? Hardly! But they did. The Scriptures state, "The people of Nineveh believed God" (Jonah 3:5a, KJV). The message must have been powerful. The Bible tells us, by implication, what Jonah preached. First, he warned the people of God's judgment (Jonah 3:4). Secondly, he preached repentance (Jonah 3:8). Thirdly, the prophet declared God's compassion. "Salvation is of the LORD" (Jonah 3:9). That kind of preaching in the power of the Spirit guarantees a response. The Bible says the Ninevites "proclaimed a fast, and put on sackcloth, from the greatest of them even to the least of them" (Jonah 3:5b, KJV). The leaders of the city commanded: "Let man and beast be covered with sackcloth, and cry mightily unto God: yea, let them turn every one from his evil way, and from the violence that is in their hands" (Jonah 3:8, KJV). In a word, the Assyrians repented and turned to God.

Here again a basic principle of spiritual awakenings shines forth: True revival and the reception of God's forgiving grace never comes without deep and thorough repentance. Every age and time attests to this fact.

During Billy Graham's great Sydney Crusade, I was conducting an evangelistic series in Tamworth, Australia. It was a "satellite" meeting in conjunction with the Sydney Crusade. The spirit of conviction fell on many, and several found Christ. One policeman of the city, however, reacted strongly. His wife, a devoted believer, was deeply concerned for her husband. She enlisted all her Christian friends to intercede for his conversion. But he remained bitterly critical and resistant to it all. Still, they prayed on. The burdened wife urged her policeman husband to attend the crusade which was being held in a large football field. He was willing to bring her to the services, but he would have no part of it. All he could do was ridicule.

One night the officer drove his wife to the crusade, said a few curt remarks and left. He thought it all so much foolishness. But suddenly the Spirit of God fell upon him as he drove away. He returned to the meeting just as the sermon began. When the invitation was extended, he literally ran down the aisle, weeping and groaning so loudly you could virtually hear him for blocks. He fell hard on his knees before all, crying out his sins before God.

The Lord did a deep, profound work in the policeman's life. Why? Because he truly repented. That is always true in revival. The Spirit of God in free grace brings people to deep and profound repentance.

Finally, and here the forgiving grace of God radiates with such beauty, He washed away Nineveh's sins. When God saw their faith and repentance, "God repented of the evil, that he had said that he would do unto them; and he did it not" (Jonah 3:10, KJV). That is grace, and grace means forgiveness and new life. How we need a fresh grasp of what our evangelical forefathers called "the doctrines of grace." God's mercy is utterly fathomless. It reaches the depths and forgives you and me.

Conclusion

Through the years, as a professor and administrator, I have traveled through many of the labyrinths of theological thought. My ministry in theological education demands that. But through it all, I have come back to where I started decades ago, hopefully with a deeper grasp of it all. What thrills me most today centers around the beautiful truth, as the hymn writer expressed it:

My sin—O the bliss of this glorious thought:
My sin not in part, but the whole
Is nail'd to the cross and I bear it no more;
Praise the Lord,
Praise the Lord, O my soul!

That is what God does. His reviving is a revelation of grace. *He really wants to forgive our sins.*

What's That Mighty Sound?

In a Spiritual Awakening God Reveals Himself as

POWER

Therefore, "He Will Hear from Heaven."
ACTS 1–2

Introduction

"Lord, are you at this time going to restore the kingdom to Israel?" inquired Jesus' followers as they gathered on the Mount of Olives (Acts 1:6). Their eyes sparkled in anticipation. This was surely the hour they had been waiting for. The time for their Messiah to break the yoke of Roman tyranny and exalt Israel as the leading nation of the world, as in the Davidic kingdom, had surely come. But, their query proved to be a rather unperceptive question. Surely, one would think, they would have acquired a deeper insight into the nature of the kingdom than that. The disciples had been with the Lord three years; had witnessed His miracles, His teachings, the Lord's whole approach to kingdom realities. Jesus literally labored to communicate His message concerning kingdom truth. Yet, they apparently still did not grasp the immediate aspect of Christ's kingly rule. Failing to realize the present manifestation of the kingdom is essentially spiritual; they were persistent in maneuvering for an earthly version. They still struggled in the grips of traditional Judaism. They may even in some sense have been seeking to establish a little kingdom of their own. James and John had earlier sought a position of honor in the kingdom, to sit on the Lord's right hand and left when He reigns (Matthew 20:20–21).

The Lord immediately set the kingdom record straight. True, there would be the universal fulfillment of the kingdom someday. But that glorious time must wait for Jesus' Second Advent, and Jesus said, "It is not for you to know the times or seasons." The sparkle probably faded from their eyes at that word. But a new thrill, with great glory, must have filled their hearts when Jesus then declared that until the day of His re-

145

turn, "You will be my witnesses" (Acts 1:8). Jesus was simply saying that before the establishment of the kingdom on earth, His disciples were to take the Gospel to the ends of the earth. In that dramatic declaration, Jesus delivered to the church its immediate, compelling commission and working agenda. As the poet well expressed it:

> Give us a watchword for the hour,
> A thrilling word, a word of power;
> A battle-cry, a flaming breath,
> That calls to conquest or to death;
> A word to rouse the church from rest,
> To heed her Master's high behest,
> The call is given: Ye hosts arise,
> Our watchword is Evangelize!

What a phenomenal task: world evangelization! We are to carry the Gospel to every creature on earth.

Regarding the fulfillment of the Great Commission, the contemporary evangelical church has put itself on the line as it never has since the first century. We say we are going to seek *the evangelization of the world in this generation.* That "missionary watchword," as it has been termed, has challenged thousands to go millions of miles in world evangelization. A worthy goal, but can it be done?

One thing remains certain, if we are ever to see the missionary watchword fulfilled and enter the next generation without disappointment, or embarrassment, we *must* have a firm grip on the power of God, manifested in the overwhelming presence of His Holy Spirit. Without power, there will be no bold world thrust! But that is exactly what constitutes a true spiritual awakening: God revealing himself in Holy Spirit power. Our Lord shows himself as *power* in all genuine revivals. To strike a phrase from the base text of this work, in a powerful awakening, God "will hear from heaven." We have heard enough from this world and the building of earthly kingdoms by professing Christians and leaders. The time has arrived to hear God speak in power from heaven, as 2 Chronicles 7:14 promises He will.

A Pattern

A foundational "Pattern of Revival Power" is outlined and illustrated in Acts, chapters 1 and 2. If ever there was a refreshing time from the Lord, it occurred in the early days of the Jerusalem church. That period always serves as the prototype of what a powerful, awakened church ought to be. The book of Acts, as one commentator states, "is not merely a mechanical story of the journeying of Paul, or of the doings of Peter. It is intended to reveal to us the process through which Christ proceeds in new power, consequent upon the things He began to do and teach, toward the ultimate and final victory."[1] This is probably why William Barclay says, "In one sense it is true to say that the Book of Acts is the most important book in the New Testament."[2]

The early chapters of Acts, therefore, clearly demonstrate that a spiritual awakening essentially centers around the people of God experiencing normal New Testament patterns. Revival is not something mysterious, mystical, even frightening or so "other worldly" that it appears unattainable. A true awakening is far removed from the attitude of an old brother who once prayed, "Lord, revive us, but don't scare us to death when you do." No, the God of revival does not reveal himself to His people like that. Revival simply moves God's people to become fully New Testament in theology *and practice*. The old cliche has it correct: Many of our churches are so scripturally subnormal that when they experience the biblically normal, they think it is abnormal and call it "revival." Perhaps the problem is, we fall so short of the scriptural ideal that a rapid, reviving, updating of these principles comes over so dramatically it seems almost to overwhelm us. Nevertheless, a spiritual awakening can be summed up as inculcating into the very fabric of the church normal New Testament Christianity. The Jerusalem believers exemplified that divine work.

In the light of this basic premise, Acts 1–2 dramatically demonstrates six principles of moving into individual and corporate New Testament awakened church life. If these principles can be implemented in experience, God will surely reveal himself in *power* and "hear from heaven." The first principle can be expressed in the following:

God Will Hear From Heaven When the Church Acquires a Proper Evaluation of Priorities

Jesus said, "You shall be my witnesses" (Acts 1:8). According to this key verse one thing becomes very obvious: Evangelism must be first in the church's ministry priority list. Of course, winning the lost to faith in Christ does not encompass everything a local church is expected to do; there are many ministries in which to engage. However, in priority, evangelism comes first. It does not solve all problems, but it stands first. Evangelism is not all serving Christ means, but seeking the lost takes first place. Love demands other services. But in priorities, evangelism ascends to the paramount position. Of course, evangelism does not necessarily come first chronologically. As one put it, a hungry person has no ears. We may need to feed the lost before we evangelize them. And even if we never get their ear, we should feed them anyway. Our Lord expects that. But *in priority*, evangelization stands as primary. What does the Good Shepherd do when one sheep is lost? He leaves the ninety and nine and goes out into the storm after that one lost lamb (Matthew 18:12–14). What causes the Father to run—God actually running?—He runs to meet and embrace the returning prodigal (Luke 15:20). What makes the heavens rejoice? One lost sinner who repents! (Luke 15:7). As the great English Baptist preacher Richard Knill said the day he embraced Jesus Christ, "At such a time of the day, clang went every harp in heaven, for Richard Knill was born again."

What do Acts 1:8 and a multitude of other similar Bible texts really say? It seems so clear. Surely they mean God puts His premium stamp on the winning of unbelievers to His Son. One can hardly be a balanced biblical believer and come to any other conclusion. Virtually all New Testament scholars, with all brands of theology, agree the ministry of Jesus dealt primarily with kingdom salvation. Granted, there have been shallow, superficial evangelistic efforts *just like every other form of ministry*, but that does not excuse a single believer for not prioritizing evangelism in individual and shared church life. We must realize the salvation of people constitutes the most important issue the church faces.

But let it be stressed again, that does not mean other ministries have no significant place in the life of the church. There are many worthy, needed, social and family ministries in which to participate. To these we should give ourselves. The tragedy of severing evangelism from social action is deplorable. It can well be called the "great divorce." God is set against it. Witnessing should always be done in a two-fold manner: (1) by word, and (2) by deed. When H. M. Stanley finally found missionary David Livingston, and spent time with him, Stanley said, "If I had been with him any longer I would have been compelled to be a Christian, and he never spoke to me about it at all."[3]

This tragic evangelism/social action cleavage is a twentieth-century phenomenon, at least in America. Our forefathers knew nothing of it. Actually, the great social movements of the past five hundred years have, by and large, grown out of revival periods. Discerning historians agree to that fact. The greatest achievements in social betterment have almost invariably come hard on the heels of a great awakening. For example, Charles G. Finney was an ardent revivalist and at the same time a fervent abolitionist. Spurgeon, the great Gospel preacher, also built orphan homes and alms houses and a college. So did Spener, Franke, and a host of pietist giants in the past. Most great social movements found their birth among evangelicals. *But in priority of importance, evangelism surfaces first.*

Important to the concept of evangelism's priority status is the fact that Jesus said the disciples would be His witness because the Holy Spirit was about to come upon them (Acts 1:8). As yet, however, the Spirit had not fallen. Pentecost was still waiting in the wings. That may well explain the disciples' misunderstanding of the nature of the kingdom. But now the Spirit has been given and abides in all true believers; therefore, a failure to avail one's self of His fullness and power precipitates a tragic error. It can easily result in a church muddling its priorities, hence making little impact in witnessing. Many evangelical churches lose ground right there, not to mention those less evangelistic. May God hear from heaven in power and revive us, filling us with His indwelling Spirit and putting us on the trail of the lost.

Witnessing never proves easy, however. The word translated "witness" in our English Bible is the Greek term "martyr." Real witnessing comes in the context of sacrifice and suffering. Therefore, it will take more than just a realization of the priority of witnessing. That is where it begins, but there is more. For God to come to us in reviving power requires a pervasive passion.

God Will Hear From Heaven When the Church Acquires a Proper Passion

What so significantly motivated the early believers? What kindled their passion? It must have been a powerful motivation; they took the first-century Roman world by storm. Their passion so captivated the masses that they became known as those who were "turning the world upside down" (Acts 17:6, KJV). Luke, the author of Acts, answers the motivation question: "And while they [the disciples] looked steadfastly toward heaven as he [Jesus] went up, behold, two men stood by them in white apparel . . . [saying] this same Jesus, which is taken up from you into heaven, shall so come in like manner as ye have seen him go into heaven" (Acts 1:10, 11, KJV). The early Christians took the angel's word at face value; they genuinely believed the Lord would return in their day. This conviction spawned in their deepest personhood the approach of Jesus who said, "I must work the works of him that sent me, while it is day: the night cometh, when no man can work" (John 9:4, KJV). They felt their days were numbered; consequently, they served with an ardent, passionate spirit. They simply had to do what they could while they still had time.

We all know that if there is no motivation, there is no action. How to motivate our apathetic people today has become the challenging issue.

Here caution becomes the word, however. Many "motivational experts" tell us many ways to motivate believers. And people can be motivated in the energy of the human spirit. They can be "psyched up," and thus generate some activity. That approach is superficial at best, and ultimately negative in God's work. Church members soon grow immune to the pressure and refuse to do much of anything. But they can also be motivated positively. How? Only by the Holy Spirit himself laying a true burden of a lost and broken world on their heart. In the final analysis, the Spirit of God comes to the church as the motivator, and His motivation lasts. The godly young missionary David Brainerd knew this secret. See him on his knees in deep snow, wet with perspiration, coughing blood from tubercular lungs, fervently interceding for the conversion of the American Indians. He said:

> I cared not where or how I lived or what hardships I went through so that I could but gain souls for Christ. While I was asleep I dreamed of these things, and when I awoke the first thing I thought of was this great work. All of my desire was for the conversion of the heathen and my hope was in God.

And how the Holy Spirit rewarded that spirit. Brainerd gives the account of how the revival blessing fell:

> The power of God seemed to descend upon the assembly "like a rushing, mighty wind" and with an astonishing energy bore down on all before it. I stood amazed at the influence that seized the audience almost universally and could compare it to nothing more aptly than the irresistible force of a mighty torrent. . . . Almost all persons of all ages were bowed down with concern together, and scarce one was able to withstand the shock of this surprising operation.[4]

Some undiscerning historians have accused Brainerd of being neurotic. If that total dedication to evangelism is neurosis, may God send it upon all Christians.

The Laity

During revival times the passion for souls springs to life and lay involvement moves ahead at a rapid pace. In a true awakening the laity, at long last, get geared for ministry. Pastors have challenged, even begged, lay folk to give their time and energies in service and witness. As one pastor put it, "I have the biggest job on earth; I have to try to open the mouths of the people in the pew." Still, the majority of the laity seem content to be mere passive spectators. Thank God for the faithful few who do witness, but they number so few. These few will never turn the blitz of Satan as "the few" in the Battle of Britain turned the Nazi tide in World War II. *All* the people of God must get into the warfare.

We will probably never see the multitudes of laity motivated, enlisted, equipped, and sent out in ministry until an awakening comes. This does not mean the church should stop challenging them and training those who will respond. We must continue to call out the few, but the ultimate answer for lay involvement is revival, for in the final analysis the Spirit of God alone can kindle the flame for a lost world. The Holy Spirit will demonstrate His presence and power in revival and "hear from heaven" when we permit Him to make us all a people of passion. Wesley said, "Give me thirty men who love nothing but God, hate nothing but sin, and seek only the glory of God, and I will set the world on fire." The Holy Spirit can sanctify us, making us that sort of saint. And there is another principle:

God Will Hear From Heaven When the Church Acquires Proper Programs

Acts 1:15 states "In those days Peter stood up among the believers . . . and said . . . ." The verses that then follow relate how the infant church selected a new apostle. In a word, the young church began to develop an institutional, programmed life.* That pattern deepened and developed as the church met and faced new needs. Acts 6 records the instituting of new church officers and a program to meet a specific need. We see that development until the Ephesian model presents a church with apostles, prophets, evangelists, pastor-teachers, "to prepare God's people for works of service" (Ephesians 4:11–12). From these realities a principle emerges: A good structural, institutionalized, programmed church life is important. By the

---

*Some commentators have questioned the propriety of this move by the disciples. G. C. Morgan, for example, sees it as a total mistake. He feels they moved presumptuously, because God had Paul in mind for the post of the twelfth Apostle. Many also question the casting of lots to make a choice. The passage does not say they prayed about the matter, but verse 14 implies it. Regardless, Luke makes no comment positively or negatively.

Holy Spirit's presence, church becomes not only a living organism, it grows into an *organization*. All that has been related in the previous points of the general revival pattern should not be seen as minimizing the importance of church structures. We must have them. The early church did. We ought to have good programs, the best that can be devised. God's cause deserves it. Two principles dictate how church programs are to be structured.

Two Principles

First, good programs should center on felt needs. Every action the church engages in should touch the real needs of real people. If any program fails to do that, it should be buried, for it has already died. To release people from non-productive activity is a wise decision. Church members have only so much time and resource to give in service; let us see to it that it is channelled to meet genuine needs inside and outside the church.

Secondly, we must be certain we do God's work correctly, that is, according to biblical patterns. King David provides an excellent illustration on this point. In 1 Chronicles 13 we are presented with a picture of David and his excitement about his heartfelt resolve. He had decided to bring the Ark of the Covenant to Jerusalem. Seeing it was God's Ark, the project deserved the very best, so he put his mind to work on devising the best means of accomplishing his goal. The King consulted with the nations' leaders (1 Chronicles 13:1–4). They decided to build a new, expensive cart, the finest they could construct. They not only agreed on that, they decided to secure a team of oxen that had never been used before, and to enlist the best singers and praisers in Israel. Putting it all together, a procession was ordered to bring God's Ark into Jerusalem in grand style. They did it just as planned. Nothing was too good for God, they all agreed.

Everything started off well. They were proceeding marvelously. It was a grand entourage. The singers were singing and the praisers were praising. Just then the oxen stumbled and the cart rocked a bit. Something always goes a little wrong. A well-meaning, but ill-informed man by the name of

Uzza put out his hand to steady the Ark. And God smote him dead.

David was shattered and frightened (1 Chronicles 13:12). He backed out of the project posthaste, left the Ark at a nearby farm, and walked into Jerusalem depressed and defeated. What went wrong? He really did mean well!

In the following months David must have seriously read the Law, the Scriptures. He discovered God had *His own way* of transporting the Ark. The king learned that it was to be carried on the shoulders of the Levites with staves (1 Chronicles 15:13). How David missed it remains a mystery; the Ark had metal loops to put the staves through. David's ignorance cost him much embarrassment, not to mention a life lost. Instead of giving up, David tried again, this time following God's biblical guidelines. Great success followed. David, the Ark, and all Israel entered Jerusalem in triumph. Conclusion: *You must do God's work God's way* to receive God's blessings. And that way can be found primarily in the pages of the Bible.

Programs are important, but God will reveal himself in power and hear from heaven only when we do His work in His fashion, that is to say, on *scriptural principles*. And that implies, as emphasized, God's people meeting real needs of real people in real life situations and doing it all according to biblical precepts. This leads to the heart of the Day of Pentecost; the bestowing of the Holy Spirit.

God Will Hear From Heaven When the Church Acquires Proper Power

Acts 2:1–4 describes the bestowing of divine power:

> And when the day of Pentecost was fully come, they were all with one accord in one place. And suddenly there came a sound from heaven as of a rushing mighty wind, and it filled all the house where they were sitting. And there appeared unto them cloven tongues like as of fire, and it sat upon each of them. And they were all filled with the Holy Ghost, and began to speak with other tongues, as the Spirit gave them utterance (KJV).

The Day of Pentecost always loomed high in the religious life of the Jews. The Day literally meant "the fifth." The festival was held fifty days after the second day of Passover. Thus it comprised a "week of weeks." The Old Testament termed it "The Festival of Weeks." The festive time came at the close of the gathering of the harvest and commemorated that event. Thus it proved an apt time for the Spirit to fall and begin to gather in the harvest of souls (Acts 2:41).

It is important to note that the Christian Pentecost itself, with the once-for-all giving of the Spirit, cannot be historically repeated any more than the cross or resurrection of Jesus Christ can be repeated. Pentecost constituted a once-for-all event. We should not try to ape it as some seem prone to do. The Holy Spirit is now here and we do not need another Pentecost in the strict historical sense. Nevertheless, as we draw on the cross and resurrection of Jesus Christ for life, so we draw experientially on the power of the Holy Spirit given on Pentecost. God intends us to experience the ongoing power of Pentecost, namely, the divine *infilling* of the Holy Spirit whom we have all received. Make no mistake, all believers possess the Holy Spirit, but all are not necessarily experiencing His fullness of power. Yet, therein alone lies strength for effective ministry.* Fullness of the Spirit means fullness of power in ministry.

The Fullness

Charles G. Finney, most would agree, stands historically as one of America's most powerful preachers. In his *Memoirs* he described one of his potent revival season services:

> I had not preached, I should think, more than a quarter of an hour, when all at once an awful solemnity seemed to settle down upon them; the congregation began to fall from their seats in every direction, and cried for mercy. If I had a sword in each hand, I could not have cut them off their seats as fast as they fell. Indeed nearly the whole congre-

---

*Noteworthy is the fact that the church was in "one accord" (vs. 1) when God rained down His Spirit upon them. There will never be the blessings of revival until accord prevails. We must bury animosities and come together in the bond of unity and love to have God's best.

gation were either on their knees or prostrate, I would think, in less than two minutes from this first shock that fell upon them.[5]

People literally fell down at the preaching of Finney. And he was not alone in this phenomenon. Edwards, Whitefield, Wesley, and others also preached with like power. Nor was it all mere emotional excess. The Holy Spirit in power effected the phenomenon. God attended their ministry in true revival power.

At the same time, the divine power of the Holy Spirit in revival is not always bombastic. Finney also said:

> I was powerfully converted on the morning of the 10th of October, 1821. In the evening of the same day I received overwhelming baptisms [infillings] of the Holy Ghost. I found myself so endued with power from on high that a few words dropped here or there in casual conversation were the means of immediate conversions.[6]

Quiet witnessing in Holy Spirit power moves people as much as preaching that may cut them down. Our responsibility is to see to it that we ourselves and our churches live so in touch with God that the Holy Spirit can dominate, control, and thus fill us with His power (Ephesians 5:18). Without the Holy Spirit there is no power, no effectiveness, no life, nothing! As the poet put it:

A city full of churches,
Great preachers, lettered men!
Grand music, choirs and organs;
If these all fail, what then?

Good workers, eager, earnest,
Who labor hour by hour,
But where, Oh where, my brother,
Is God's almighty power?
Refinement, education!
They have the very best.
Their plans and schemes are perfect,
They give themselves no rest.

They give the best of talent,
They try their uttermost,
But what they need, my brother,
Is God, the Holy Ghost.

Charles Spurgeon on one occasion said to his great London congregation: "If we have not the Spirit of God, let us write 'Ichabod' over our door and go home and pray until we have Him." Spurgeon was right; if we have no power we need revival.

One day I had the privilege of sitting in a small room at the great Spurgeon's Tabernacle in London, England. My heart burned within me. I felt I was having one of the spiritual treats of my Christian experience. The story begins over fifty years earlier—in East Africa.

The East African Revival

Bishop Butler of the Church of England was ministering with reasonable results in an East African work known as the Rwanda Mission. In that context, God gave the good bishop a profound burden for better things, for real revival. He prayed as if he would not be denied. As the burden and need deepened, revival winds began gently to blow. Soon the entire Rwanda Mission found itself lifted high on the wings of the "mighty rushing wind." Tens of thousands came to Christ. One of the outstanding early converts of the awakening was a native by the name of William Uganda. God called him to preach and touched his lips with coals of fire from off the altar. He preached with such power that multitudes experienced salvation. He radiated the presence and love and power of God. Soon the awakening swept all East Africa.

One of the amazing aspects of the African revival centered in the unusual length of the movement. When I first heard of it in the early 1950s, it had already been flowering for over twenty years. Norman Grubb, the man of God through whom I learned of the movement, wrote a book on the work under the title *Continuous Revival*—it was well named. The Holy Spirit worked in revival power for decades.

What perpetuated the revival for so long a period was epitomized in three key words that became the core of the movement: openness, brokenness, and challenge.

Openness: open and honest confession of one's sins, realizing sin alone slays the spirit of revival.
Brokenness: broken over sin and the loss of fellowship with God and others.
Challenge: challenging fellow believers to a moment-by-moment walk with the Lord.

The way these principles worked out in the context of the awakening proved fascinating. As the believers met day by day they would challenge each other with the question, "Is your cup running over?" That question immediately put one on the spot. If he or she did not have a "running over cup," a life filled with the joy and peace of Christ, it was because of unforsaken, unconfessed sin. So they either had to own up to their unconfessed sin, or lie. This challenge usually brought about openness concerning their sin and brokenness over it. Thus, they were challenged to confess their sin and seek the restoration of joy. Then they would sing a little chorus on the power of the blood of Christ to cleanse.

In this fashion the revival was perpetuated on a daily basis. In the final analysis, revival is really no more than an ongoing, vibrant, Spirit-filled fellowship with Jesus Christ (1 John 1:1–9). The simple exercise kept the fellowship alive and the fellowship kept the revival going. The awakening continued until the tragedy of the reign of terror by Ide Amin, in which he slaughtered thousands of Christians. After the overthrow of this bloody monarch, the revival flared up again. Today, the evangelical church is growing in East Africa three times as fast as the population growth. And remember, Africa is in the midst of the population explosion.

That meeting in Spurgeon's Tabernacle in which I was involved, was with Bishop Butler and William Uganda themselves. I shall never forget the encounter. It proved to be one of my first experiences of fellowship with someone God had used significantly in a true spiritual awakening. For me it became a "mini-revival" in itself. The power of God rested powerfully on these men. I will never forget William Uganda. He looked at us all, and simply said, "I love you." I cannot explain how profoundly all were touched by those three words. The Holy Spirit truly had shed abroad in his heart the love of God (Romans 5:5). But a true manifestation of the love of God always forms a major part of a Holy Spirit revival. It profoundly moved me and deepened my desire to one day see an awakening dawn in my life and ministry.

From where did all that love, power, evangelism, and dynamic spirituality stem? From the only source that it can arise: The mighty presence of the Holy Spirit as He dominates, fills, and makes the lives of believers powerful for God. The question for a people desiring revival invariably becomes: Are we "filled with the Spirit?" (Ephesians 5:18). The issue of Pentecost is not where are the tongues, the fire, and the wind. The real issue is always, where is the mighty power of the Holy Spirit to convict the lost, sanctify the saints, and bring about holiness of life to the greater glory of God by revealing Jesus Christ. That epitomizes His real work: to reveal the Lord Christ, and that is revival (John 15:26). In all our getting, may we permit the Spirit to point us to Jesus and thus experience His powerful *presence* among us. Without His constant work, we soon loose all that is vital in individual and corporate church life. And how do we "get Him"? Of course, all believers are indwelt by the Holy Spirit. So, actually, the real question is: How does He get us? The answer is simple: The Bible says God has given the Holy Spirit "to those who *obey* him" (Acts 5:32). There rests the prime principle. We are to be absolutely surrendered to the Holy Spirit to receive His fullness and power. Then by faith we claim His fullness. Committal and faith are the key.

But there is a fifth principle that needs at least brief mentioning. It, too, becomes essential in revival. It must be considered, albeit the principle does not directly apply to all Christians. It is a word to preachers of the Gospel. But often the key to revival rests in the preacher's hands. It can be expressed as:

God Will Hear From Heaven When the Church Acquires Proper Preaching

Pure biblical preaching assumes a major role in a great awakening. Peter's sermon recorded in Acts 2:14–40 makes this principle plain. The Gospel ever remains "the power of God unto salvation" (Romans 1:18), and great preachers preach it in purity, simplicity, and power. But where are the giants of the pulpit today? The humorous critic rightly expressed our contemporary preaching problem:

> I never see my preacher's eyes,
> Regardless how they shine.
> For when he prays he closes his
> And when he preaches, mine.

This little quip actually poses a serious situation, for the health curve of the church parallels powerful, biblical preaching. The reaction of church attenders regarding their pastors is too often a confession that the sermons they hear are dull. As someone said, "If the church is ever found assassinated, the dagger in its back will be the poor sermon." Pastors, evangelists, missionaries, preachers, ought to preach the full Word of God, and do it with zeal and Holy Spirit power. There will be found no dullness or lifelessness in the church if it experiences inspired preaching.

Two thoughts are important here. First, preaching in the power of the Holy Spirit assumes a vital place in the service of Christ for preachers. Other ministries have their place, but the preaching of the Word should have prominence. Preaching in God's power brings life and vitality. Secondly, the fearless preaching of the simple Gospel pleases God most highly and brings glorious results. But be sure the message is the Word of the Gospel, not humanistic reasoning or mere emotional appeals. It was not the nails and hammer the reformer Martin Luther used on that great day, October 31, 1517, that caused the worldwide impact of the 95 Theses he nailed on the Wittenburg church door. Rather, it was the *truth* of the Theses that made the difference. Paul said, "And my speech and my preaching was not with enticing words of man's wisdom, but in demonstration of the Spirit and of power" (1 Corinthians 2:4, KJV). Preaching of the whole truth of the Bible in Holy Spirit power is what God blesses and honors. God crowns that effort with conversions. The Gospel explodes with power. And what makes up that simple yet most profound message of the Gospel? The sermon of Peter on the Day of Pentecost presents the essential truths.

The Gospel

Bible scholars, such as C. H. Dodd, have labored over the nature of the Gospel. Most conclude that the proclamation of Christ (the *kerygma*, cf. 1 Corinthians 1:21) has several major points:

1. Jesus is the long-awaited Messiah (Acts 2:36).
2. He lived a perfect life—teaching, healing, etc. (Acts 2:22).
3. He died in our place on the cross for our sins (Acts 2:23).
4. He bodily arose from the grave (Acts 2:24).
5. In the light of all this, people are to repent and exercise faith (Acts 2:38).
6. If they respond positively they have the promise of forgiveness and salvation (Acts 2:38).*

All these points Peter presented in power. They should be the contemporary preachers' message when they attempt to evangelize. These salient truths become the essence of all witnessing, personal or from the pulpit. When Christ is faithfully proclaimed, we discover with Paul that the Gospel truly is the "power of God" (Romans 1:17).

The list of the pulpit giants whom God used to spawn revival by their great preaching is endless. History still records the powerful proclamation of men like John Chrysostom, Luther, Calvin, Baxter, Bunyan, Wesley, Whitefield, Edwards, Spurgeon, Alexander Maclaren, Finney, and others. The whole world, not to mention our own church people, are languishing for Spirit-endued, biblical, expository preaching. Heavenly preaching brings heavenly power. My personal plea to preachers is to be a powerful expositor of the Word. When we preachers end our ministry, may we be able to say with Paul: "Wherefore I take you to record this day, that I am pure from the blood of all men. For I have not shunned to declare to you all the counsel of God" (Acts 20:26–27, KJV).

Of course, the same simple Gospel is what all believers are to share. As it applies to preaching, it also applies to all in witnessing for Christ. No Christian should be without knowl-

*See C. H. Dodd, *The Apostolic Preaching and Its Development,* Michael Green, *Evangelism in the Early Church,* and James Stewart, *A Faith to Proclaim.* These are just a sampling of works on the *kerygma,* or "Gospel."

edge of the message of Christ. God uses the truth to bring people to His Son. Finally, and most important of all:

God Will Hear From Heaven When the Church Provides Proper Prayer

The real root of Pentecost is found in chapter 1, verse 14 of Acts. In that verse we discover the ultimate key to revival: "These all continued with one accord in prayer and supplication." As has already been stressed time and again, prayer forms the foundation of every spiritual awakening. Intercession strikes the downbeat that sets the heavenly choir singing. But notice, with "one accord" the seekers prayed. Unity is vital to effective prayer, and that quality of corporate prayer becomes essential if we are to have real revival. Acts 4:32–33 tells us: "The company of those who believed were of one heart and soul . . . and with great power the Apostles gave their testimony to the resurrection of the Lord Jesus and great grace was upon them all." Unity and power and grace entwine themselves in effectual praise for spiritual awakening. Charles G. Finney put it correctly when he said:

> Prayer is an essential link in the chain of courses that lead to revival. In regard to my own experience, I will say that unless I had the spirit of prayer I would do nothing. If even for a day or an hour I lost the spirit of grace and supplication, I found myself unable to preach with power and efficiency, or to win souls.

Most fortunately the number of those who are burdened for revival, and will therefore sacrificially pray, need not be many. History tells us a small handful can precipitate a genuine awakening. Herman Humphrey in *Revival Sketches* relates how revival came to Hampden-Sydney College of Virginia in 1782. He stated:

> Four students decided to hold a prayer meeting in one of the dormitory rooms. They tried to be as quiet about it as possible, but were discovered. So much commotion was caused that the matter came to the attention of the president, Dr. John Blair Smith. With tears in his eyes he said, "Oh, is there such a state of things in this college? You shall

hold your next meeting in my parlor, and I will be one of your number." The next meeting was indeed held in the president's parlor and half the college was present. There began a glorious revival which pervaded the college and spread into the surrounding area.

Jacob's Prayer

In the end, our choice inevitably becomes that which Jacob the patriarch faced as he returned from Haran to his father Isaac. Jacob had to decide if he was going to serve God on a "human" or on a "divine" level. So must we. The decision for us all is always whether to be a "Jacob" or an "Israel," as it were. The story is recorded in Genesis 32. Prayer became the crux of the matter.

The account begins when Jacob was still some distance from his home. He had been gone many years. He had built his own kingdom with flocks, children, wives, and wealth. He had become a good personal kingdom builder; even prior to his leaving home he had wrestled the birthright and blessing from his twin brother Esau. These incidents forced his trip to Haran in the first place. Esau vowed to kill him over the matter. Jacob excelled as a real manipulator. His very name "Jacob" means "a crafty one." Yet, he was a believer. He had had his Bethel experience. Nonetheless, so much of Jacob's experience seemed very humanistic.

Now, however, the crunch had come. A scouting servant galloped back into camp with shattering news. He cried out to Jacob, "Your brother, Esau, is riding hard this way with 400 armed men." Jacob almost collapsed with fear. He could visualize 400 wild, revengeful Arabs riding like fury toward his camp. "Oh, why did I ever cheat my brother out of the birthright and blessing," Jacob shuddered. But then, "Jacob," the "crafty one," took over. *Now let me plan a crafty way to placate my brother,* he thought. He was living up to his name. So he put his humanistic ways into full action. He arranged three sets of gifts and sent them ahead to Esau. Then he divided his family into lots and sent them on. Maybe by the time that wild band gets through the gifts and sees the family, Esau will be softened, Jacob reasoned. But will it work? Jacob trembled. The panicked Jacob prayed: "Oh, God, help, help. I'm not worthy, but help" (Genesis 32:9–12). He did have a measure of faith. Finally, Jacob came to the end of "Jacob," and the Scriptures tell us he put his wives and children over the Jabbok stream and alone, for the first time, really came to grips with himself—and God.

On the other side of the stream, the Bible says Jacob met *a man*. But He was not a "man" at all. God wrestled with Jacob that night.

"Let me go," cried the *Man*.

"No," cried Jacob. "Not until you bless me."

"Let me go!"

"No."

"Let me go!"

"No, I will not let you go unless you bless me," cried the anguished Jacob.

"If you do not let me go," cried the Man, "I will smite you and you will limp through life."

"Smite me, I'll be a cripple—Smite me, I will not let you go until you bless me." Jacob hung on and God smote him, and for the rest of his life he did limp.

Then God said, "What is your name?" Of course, God knew it; He wanted Jacob to know it.

"My name is Jacob; the 'supplanter,' 'the crafty one.' Yes, that is my name, and that's what I am," Jacob acknowledged.

"No," said God. "You are no longer Jacob, you are now *Israel*; one who wrestles and prevails with God. A kingdom of power is yours. The blessing and birthright are yours, *Israel. You have prevailed.*"

The drama closes as the rising sun sheds its first rays over the eastern horizon. Silhouetted on the top of a sand dune stands Israel and his brother Esau embraced in reconciliation. Prayer truly changes things.

Conclusion

What will it be for us in our quest for a spiritual awakening? Will we be a "Jacob" or an "Israel," one who prevails with God. Revival victory grows out of wrestling with God, that is, wrestling in fervent prayer. Heavenly power lies there, and there alone. We may limp through life, but we will prevail. People may not understand, but we will prevail. We may not do as we once did, but we will prevail. Jacob or Israel? Which shall it be? Make no mistake, God reveals himself in reviving power and "hears from heaven" only through *Israelites*! And that is New Testament Christianity.

From "Ichabod" to "Ebenezer"

In a Spiritual Awakening God Reveals Himself as
LOVE

Therefore, He Will "Heal our Land."
1 SAMUEL 4–7

Introduction

"Ichabod"—a disturbing word! "The glory is departed." A disturbing situation: God is gone. How could it have come to this? When the affair started, the Israelites never dreamed it possible. Was not God always to be with them? Their whole history attested to that reality. What does it all mean, this "Ichabod" scene?

Ichabod in America

But then, right after the birth of the United States, neither did the early American spiritual fathers realize what could occur when an "Ichabod" situation settles in. The glory of God had fallen upon them decades earlier during what historians call the "First Great Awakening." In 1734, that magnificent movement was born when the scholarly young pastor, Jonathan Edwards, began preaching with new power to the people of Northampton, Massachusetts. His grandfather, Solomon Stoddard, who preceded him as pastor, experienced four significant revivals in his effective ministry. But when Edwards came to the Northampton pulpit, the Puritan community needed another fresh touch from God. The so-called "Half-Way Covenant"* put many unregenerate people on the roles of the churches in New England, thus diluting

---

*This arrangement permitted lost people to have their children baptized and become church members. However, these children could not partake of the Lord's Supper until they professed conversion. Nevertheless, it put many people in church membership who did not truly know Christ. Rather strangely, Solomon Stoddard had advocated the Half-Way Covenant. Edwards strongly disagreed.

the congregations' Christian witness. The concerned, regenerate believers began to pray. In 1734 the fire of heaven fell, especially upon the young people. The glow then subsided somewhat for six years. But in the early 1740s the eloquent George Whitefield traveled to New England from London and the full revival broke. Whitefield could sway the masses unbelievably. Benjamin Franklin calculated Whitefield could be heard distinctly and clearly in the open air by over 30,000 people. Franklin profoundly admired the English evangelist and they became good friends.

In those days of revival power, it seemed as if Jonathan Edwards and George Whitefield joined hands and reached the whole eastern seaboard of America for Jesus Christ. Through their preaching, thousands came to Christ as God mightily awakened His church. Those were the glory years.

Edwards and Whitefield contrasted each other rather dramatically. Edwards was almost an intellectual recluse. He studied over eight hours every day. He read his sermons from a full manuscript. His handwriting was poor and his eyesight matched his penmanship. He would bury his face in his manuscript, rarely looking at his congregation as he preached. What a picture he presented in the pulpit, preaching "Sinners in the Hands of an Angry God," never looking up at the people while they writhed in conviction, some even falling to the floor under the grip of the Holy Spirit.

Whitefield was the antithesis. A bout with measles in his youth left him with a squinting left eye; his detractors called him Dr. Squintum. But he possessed such natural eloquence and beautiful flow of English that the squinting eye was soon forgotten. He has never been excelled in pulpit oratory; probably equaled only by C. H. Spurgeon. David Garrick, the great British actor of the time, said Whitefield could reduce an audience to tears by merely saying the word "Mesopotamia." Whitefield traveled to America seven times, died on his last trip, and is today buried in a little crypt under the pulpit of the old Presbyterian Church of Newburyport, Massachusetts. How different the two were, but remember, in revival God uses all sorts of saints.

During the harvest season of America's First Awakening, God reaped the country in such a moving manner that "glory filled the land" (Psalms 85:9). Surely the nation could never be "Ichabod" again—at least so they thought. But the Revolutionary War came and went, and with it the revival rains dried up, the heavens became brass and the land spiritually shriveled into a dry desert. As J. Edwin Orr pointed out, by the year 1785, just 40 years after the peak of the revival:

> In the wake of the American Revolution there was a moral slump. Drunkenness became epidemic. Out of a population of five million, 300,000 were confirmed drunkards: They were burying fifteen thousand of them each year. Profanity was of the most shocking kind. For the first time in the history of the American settlement, women were afraid to go out at night for fear of assault. Bank robberies were a daily occurrence.
>
> What about the churches? The Methodists were losing more members than they were gaining. The Baptists said that they had their most wintry season. The Presbyterians in general assembly deplored the nation's ungodliness. In a typical Congregational church, the Rev. Samuel Shepherd of Lennox, Massachusetts in sixteen years had not taken one young person into fellowship. The Lutherans were so languishing that they discussed uniting with Episcopalians, who were even worse off. The Protestant Episcopal Bishop of New York, Bishop Samuel Provoost, quit functioning; he had confirmed no one for so long that he decided he was out of work, so he took up other employment. The Chief Justice of the United States, John Marshall, wrote to the Bishop of Virginia, James Madison, that the church "was too far gone ever to be redeemed." Voltaire averred, and Tom Paine echoed, "Christianity will be forgotten in thirty years."
>
> In case this is thought to be the hysteria of the moment, Kenneth Scott Latourette, the great church historian, wrote: "It seemed as if Christianity were about to be ushered out of the affairs of men." The churches had their backs to the wall, seeming as if they were about to be wiped out.[1]

What had happened? The answer is simple, the Glory had departed: Ichabod. But had God truly gone? Was it all over? No, for God in revival reveals himself as *love*; and love suffers long, never forsaking, constantly abiding. Our Lord always seeks in love to "heal the land," as Solomon promised in our 2 Chronicles text. There resides in the depths of God's love an "Ebenezer," a "stone of help," to stir the church to revival. God's reviving love invariably undergirds His people in that upward climb. The possibility of moving from "Ichabod" (1 Samuel 4:21) to "Ebenezer" (1 Samuel 7:12) forever remains the promise of spiritual awakening as it flows out of the fathomless love of the Father. How does that grand move come about? First, we must realize that in a genuine spiritual awakening, the love of God can never be finally frustrated.

No Condition Contradicts God's Reviving Love

Patent is the fact that a person, a church, a whole denomination, the entire religious moral life of a nation can dramatically deteriorate, as we have seen. Immorality can engulf and destroy a society. Institutionalism and an attending apathy can conquer any church and drain the dynamic from that which once vibrated with vitality. Individuals and entire congregations can easily turn in on themselves and begin to exist for their own existence. God's people can descend the same steps as did ancient Israel under the priesthood of Eli and his sons. A vicious spiritual spiral ensues, ending in "Ichabod." The descending stairway is described in 1 Samuel, chapters three and four.

Step One: No powerful, visionary preaching. In 1 Samuel 3:1 it states, "The word of the LORD was rare in those days; there was no frequent vision" (RSV). Much preaching and much prophesying, but no *real* word from the Lord emerged. Many ideas and schemes and plans and programs were tried, but no "frequent visions" could be discovered. That scenario forms the initial step toward decline. When true spiritual power fails, reliance on mere programming and ritualism always seems to develop. And inevitably, the true spiritual vision fades. The liturgy gets as rigid as concrete—and as impervious to the spiritual refreshing rains. Then comes the decay that erodes away the moral foundations. Eli's sons, the priests, were corrupt to the core. Eli failed to correct his sons, and they prostituted the nation. As one commentator put it, "Rarely has immorality, unjustice, and corruption of every sort achieved greater freedom."[2] Such degeneration always leads to the next step of decline.

Step Two: The beginning of defeat. The shout echoed throughout the land, "The Philistines are coming. To battle, O Israel." But that should have been no problem for Israel; they were God's people. Maybe no vision could be found, but they still professed Yahweh. Perhaps no recent word for the Lord had been heard, but they were the chosen people. The poor deluded Israelites settled down in their supposed security, and presumptuously strode out to do battle with the Philistines. They failed to realize their dire poverty of spirit. That inevitably leads to humanistic religious pride, and "pride goes before destruction, a haughty spirit before a fall" (Proverbs 16:18). In 1 Samuel 4:2 we see the devastating results: "Israel was defeated by the Philistines, who killed about four thousand men of them on the battlefield" What a startling shock that must have been. How could those who profess Yahweh be defeated? How could the covenant people be so humiliated? Tragically, the slaughter did not lead them to repentance. It did not break their heart and force them to lift their eyes to the Lord. "Ichabod" was now seriously setting in, which led Israel to their next move.

Step Three: Rationalization. The elders held a council meeting. They asked, "Wherefore hath the LORD smitten us today before the Philistines?" (1 Samuel 4:3, KJV). They began to seek some answers. Some probably said, "Well, let's not get too disturbed, we only lost 4,000 men. It could have been worse." We hear some say the same thing today: "True, we have many churches reporting few conversions this past year, but it could have been worse." What a sad rationalization when well over thirty million people die every year in our contemporary world who have never even once heard the Good News of Jesus Christ.

Others of the Israelites were emotionally upset, but not truly *spiritually* disturbed. "What to do," they cried. "Why did God permit this? We need to get God among us again." Right then they made an even more tragic mistake than the rationalizers. They attempted to get God in their midst by their own humanistic devices. In their shallow, superstitious understanding of the faith, they visualized God's presence as being in and around the Ark of the Covenant. They actually thought they had God in that box. Alexander Maclaren said,

173

"They had not learned the ABC's of their history."[3] With their superstitious belief in how to retrieve God's Presence, they said, "Let us bring the ark of the covenant of the LORD here from Shiloh, that he may come among us and save us from the power of our enemies" (1 Samuel 4:3, RSV). How presumptuous! No one except the high priest had the privilege to enter the Holy of Holies and look at the Ark, let alone remove it. Their act was more than mere presumption; it was actually idolatrous. They made an idol of the Ark. God never honors that. If only Samuel, the real man of God had been there, it might have been different. But at that stage of deterioration, they were not of a mind to hear God's true prophet. So they marched out to battle with the Ark in their ranks. Their shallow, superstitious, presumptuous, idolatrous faith precipitated the next tragic step.

Step Four: A real defeat. We read in 1 Samuel 4:10: "And the Philistines fought, and Israel was smitten, and they fled every man into his tent: and there was a very great slaughter; for there fell of Israel thirty thousand footmen" (KJV). Thirty thousand mutilated corpses lay strewn all over the battlefield. The ground was red with blood. Widows and fatherless children wept. The elders tore their robes and beat their chests. The people were in a total panic. Israel was down, defeated, and routed. Eli broke his neck, and his two priest sons were slain. What seemed like the end was surpassed by one final blow.

Step Five: The Ark of God was captured (1 Samuel 4:11). The Ark of the Covenant was lost. That really was the end. The Philistines had "captured God." Little wonder when Eli's daughter-in-law in the turmoil of it all gave an untimely birth and called the child "Ichabod," the "glory has departed." It had! The glory of Israel did not center in their geographical size, their political influence, their great armies, their abounding wealth, even their superficial spirituality. Israel's glory was the *presence of God*. And now, at least in their understanding, they had lost that. Actually, they had lost God's presence long before they lost the Ark. God's power went when they refused to repent and turn to God. That is what Ichabod is all about.

As we look at our "land," i.e., our churches (the contem-

174

porary parallel to Israel is *not* America, Britain, or any nation; rather, it is the *church*), we are forced to confess that many of our congregations really seem to be Ichabod, the glory departed. A church's glory does not rest in big budgets, beautiful buildings, liturgy, or a multitude of members or well-planned programs. A church's glory is the *presence of God*.

Is God *really* among us? That is the question. So often the Philistines appear to have routed us in the battle for souls. How our own "land" needs to be healed! It seems so long since we have had a real touch from God. Are the promises of 2 Chronicles 7:14 true? Can God actually heal our Ichabod situation, our Ichabod churches, our Ichabod lives, and move us to an "Ebenezer" revival? Yes, for God still loves us. God always reveals himself as love in a spiritual awakening and will "heal our land." This is true because God is never ultimately defeated.

No Defeat Can Destroy God's Reviving Love

Behind every tragic Ichabod incident God labors to heal our land, not just our churches but our entire country. God loves the whole world, even the "Philistines" who battle the church. But God often works very quietly, quietly to us, that is, in the general world scene. We may be oblivious to what is really going on among the contemporary "Philistines," but God works nonetheless. What the Philistines of Samuel's day experienced when they took the captured Ark and set it up in the temple of their god Dagon can perhaps give us a little insight as to how God does His works among the "Philistines" of our day.

Yahweh and Dagon

First, Dagon suffers a crushing defeat. False gods finally fail. In fact, the scene is almost humorous. Proud Dagon, the Philistines' god, perched high in splendor on his pedestal, suddenly falls on his face before the Ark of God (1 Samuel 5:3a). All the "gods" of this world will one day be prostrated before the splendor of the true and living God. They ought to fall, for no "Dagon" can meet our deep human needs. Nothing can fill the "God-shaped vacuum" in the human heart except Jesus Christ (John 10:10). But so often the world fails to realize that, so they struggle and muddle on, trying to find a meaningful life in their own "god."

The Philistines were resourceful, however. They put Dagon back up (1 Samuel 5:3b). After all, this kind of god needs all the help he can get from his devotees. But the next day, "When they arose early on the morrow morning, behold, Dagon was fallen upon his face to the ground before the ark of the LORD; and the head of Dagon and both the palms of his hands were cut off upon the threshold; only the stump of Dagon was left to him" (1 Samuel 5:4, KJV). That finally put Dagon in his proper place. God was trying to say something to the poor benighted idol worshipers.

The point is, God works far more dynamically among the "Philistines" out there than we in the church may ever imagine. God loves them, and judges them to bring them to their senses as to who the true God is and who alone can create a meaningful life. Tragically, the Philistines in this particular historical incident failed to get the message. The defeat of Dagon and plague of tumors did not move these heathen to worship the true God. When a people reject God, His presence then becomes a presence of judgment, not blessing. Therefore, all they wanted to do was get rid of the symbol of His presence. Not everyone comes to Christ regardless of God's moving among them. Yet, He still loves them and yearns to see them come to himself, even if they reject that loving revelation. It is the Father's will that none perish (2 Peter 3:9).

In the meantime, back in Israel, God was even more profoundly at work. Again, the Spirit moved in a rather quiet way at first. Their hearts were apparently so cold and hard, God could not do a sweeping work right at the outset. He started His work of grace by preparing a prophet. It all began with a small boy in the tabernacle. The story of Samuel's rise to be God's spokesman spins a thrilling tale.

After Hannah dedicated her little son Samuel to God, the Lord molded that young life into His likeness until, finally, we read: "All Israel from Dan to Beer-sheba knew that Samuel was established as a prophet of the LORD" (1 Samuel 3:20, RSV). The Lord had His hand on the fledgling prophet in such a fashion that, as the Bible says, "The LORD was with him [Samuel] and let none of his words fall to the ground" (1 Samuel 3:19, RSV). God prepared His man to stand in the breach when the dam broke. Historian James Burns' principle "the emergence of the prophet" suddenly surfaced. Why? Because God in revival love, through His servant Samuel, was about "to heal the land." And when God's hour comes, regardless of the depth of the Ichabod situation, nothing can terminally hinder our Lord's reviving work no matter how hard and calloused His people may have become.

No Hardness of Heart Hinders God's Reviving Love

The Spirit of God searches the whole earth, trying to find some servant to meet the spiritual conditions of revival, especially the condition of prevailing prayer. In love He will eventually ferret out some sincere handful to pay the price of reviving intercession. God will not allow Ichabod to be written over His people forever. *He will "heal our land."* At the age of 80, Benjamin Franklin, hardly an evangelical Christian, nonetheless put his finger on it at the Continental Congress when he said, "I have lived, sirs, a long time, and the longer I live the more convincing proofs I see of this truth, that God governs in the affairs of men."*

In Israel's case, it took the Jews twenty years of lamenting after the Lord before God mightily came among them again: "And it came to pass, while the ark abode in Kirjathjearim, that the time was long; for it was twenty years: and all the house of Israel lamented after the LORD" (1 Samuel 7:2, KJV). It took twenty years of slavery and oppression by the godless, brutal Philistines; twenty years with no visible evidence of God's presence; twenty years of tears and remorse; twenty years of lamenting after God. The Ark was gone. The image presented in the striking word "lamented" pictures a

---

*One wonders how influential George Whitefield was in Franklin's spiritual perceptions. Whitefield labored to win Franklin to Christ, but apparently unsuccessfully. Nevertheless, Franklin greatly admired Whitefield and no doubt was impacted by his life.

child weeping and sobbing after its parents that they may relieve the hurt and pain. And it demands "lamenting after the LORD" to experience the Lord's healing, reviving love. The principle that shines forth clearly is the fact that the burdened ones are those who receive revival blessings and thus become the source of awakening blessings for others. When God's people deeply and sincerely lament after God, revival is assured. The preaching and prayers of Samuel were doing their redemptive work.

The Revival in China

That is exactly what happened in the great awakening in China, in 1906, under the preaching-praying ministry of missionary Jonathan Goforth. One of the greatest revivals in the Far East occurred during the significant missionary ministry of "Goforth of China," as he was called. In his significant book *By My Spirit*, he recounts the dramatic day when revival broke in China. It all began by a purging in his own life. Goforth tells the dramatic story:

> In the autumn of 1906, having felt depressed for some time by the cold and fruitless condition of my out-stations, I was preparing to set out on a tour to see what could be done to revive them. There was a matter, however, between the Lord and myself, that had to be straightened out before He could use me. I need not go into the details. Suffice to say that there was a difference between a brother missionary and myself. . . .
>
> "But Lord," I expostulated, "he came to my study and in tears confessed his fault. So, isn't the thing settled?" "You hypocrite!" I seemed to hear Him say, "you know that you are not loving each other as brethren, as I commanded you to."
>
> The night before I was to start out on my trip I had to lead the prayer meeting for the Chinese Christians. All the way out to the church the pressure continued: "Go and straighten this thing out, so that I may go with you tomorrow." I promised in my heart, "as soon as this meeting is over, I'll go and make that matter right."
>
> It was late that night when the meeting closed. As soon as I could get away I hastened over to the house of my

brother missionary, only to find that the lights were out and that the whole family were in bed. Not wishing to disturb them I went back to my home. But the difficulty was settled. Next morning, before daybreak, I was on my way to the first out-station. The results of that tour far exceeded anything that I had dared hope for. . . . Wrongs were righted and crooked things were made straight. At one place I was only able to spend a single night, but that night all present broke down.[4]

The fire fell again two years later in February 1908, in the city of Mukden. During the early days of Goforth's ministry in Mukden, however, things did not look too promising. Goforth had stipulated two conditions to his acceptance of a series of meetings in the city. One, the two branches of the Presbyterian Church in town, the Scottish and Irish, should unite for the services; and two, the way should be paved by much prayer. Neither condition had been met when the missionary arrived. He said he went to his room and prayed, "What is the use of my coming here? These people are not seeking after thee. They have no desire for blessing. What can I do?" A word from the Lord seemed to come back, "Call unto Me and I will answer thee, and shew thee great and mighty things, which thou knowest not" (Jeremiah 33:3, KJV).

The very next morning, an elder of the church came to Goforth. As they conversed the elder suddenly burst out weeping. He confessed that as treasurer of the church he had stolen funds. In the terrible Boxer Rebellion at the turn of the century, all the account books of the church were destroyed. Consequently, he had opportunity to steal, and he did. But broken, he cried out, "Last night I couldn't sleep a wink. It has been made plain to me that the only way I can find relief is to confess my sin before the church and make full restitution." The convicting work of the Spirit had begun in spite of the dilatory church. God reigns in revival and His love can break stubborn hearts.

After Goforth's morning address that day, the elder came forward and laid bare his sin before the entire congregation. That was quite appropriate; he had sinned against them all (James 5:16). Goforth said, "The effect was instantaneous." Suddenly a man in the back of the building uttered a piercing cry, but then seemed to hold back and seal his lips. Rather strange! Nevertheless, many others were moved to tears and followed one another in prayer pouring out their confessions. For three days the convicting work deepened in intensity. One of the resident missionaries remarked, "This amazes us. It is just like the Scottish Revival of 1859."

The fourth day, after a personal spiritual battle, Goforth arose to speak. But all he could do was beg the people to pray. Immediately a man came forward, tears streaming down his cheeks. It was the man who on the first evening had let out the piercing cry but had withdrawn and said nothing. Now, completely broken, he poured out his heart, "I have committed adultery. I have tried three times to poison my wife." And he was an elder in the church. Taking out his elder's card, he tore it up, threw the fragments on the floor and cried, "I have disgraced the holy office. I herewith resign my eldership."

A deadly hush fell over the congregation. No one moved or spoke. They sat there as stone statues. Then slowly, one after another, the entire group of elders and all the deacons rose and likewise confessed their utter unworthiness to serve in the high office and proffered their respective resignations. Even the native pastor arose and resigned his office. He said, "It is I who am to blame. If I had been what I ought to have been, this congregation would not be where it is today. I am not fit to be your pastor any longer. I, too, must resign." Then a spontaneous outflow of love from the congregation arose. They would not accept any of the resignations. They all cried, "We appoint you to be our pastor. We appoint you all to be our elders and deacons." Perfect harmony and trust flooded the scene as fellowship was beautifully restored.

Then came the evangelistic explosion. The revived church moved into a deep concern for the lost. As Goforth put it:

> The whole audience stood up as one man and united in prayer for the lost sheep. They prayed as if the souls of those wandering ones were the only things that mattered. It was like a mother pleading for the return of her rebellious son. That year hundreds of members, who had drifted away, returned to the fold. Most of them confessed that they did not think that they had ever really been converted before.[5]

The awakening soon spread to the nearby city of Leaoyan,

and what God did there became the emanating source of a movement that spread throughout the whole surrounding country. Bands of revived Christians traveled far and wide sharing Christ with powerful effect. A glorious revival ensued. God had raised an "Ebenezer" awakening for those blessed Chinese people, as He did for Israel centuries earlier.

Israel's Three Steps to "Ebenezer"

There are always three significant steps that lead from Ichabod to Ebenezer, as the Chinese and Israel before them discovered.

Repentance. Samuel said, "If ye do return unto the LORD with all your hearts, then put away the strange gods and Ashtaroth from among you, and prepare your hearts unto the LORD, and serve him only: and he will deliver you out of the hand of the Philistines" (1 Samuel 7:3, KJV). There can be no competing loyalties with God. You either serve God or mammon (Matthew 6:24). Notice how Samuel specifically mentioned Ashtaroth idol worship. Turning from specific sins is demanded in real repentance. The worship of Ashtaroth was the darling of the apostate Jews. God always puts His finger on our "darling" sin. God will never return the "Ark" until there is honest confession and forsaking and putting right specific areas of rebellion. The Israelites even fasted, so sincere was their repentance (1 Samuel 7:6). That commitment enabled them to "fix their hearts on God" and "serve Him only" (1 Samuel 7:30). This act of repentance was twofold. It first meant getting one's eyes off sin— which constitutes the negative side, and secondly, looking to God, the positive side of real repentance. A deep rejection of sin and renewed focus on God will result in dedicated, sincere service.

Prayer. First Samuel 7:7–8 states, "The children of Israel . . . were afraid of the Philistines. And the children of Israel said to Samuel, Cease not to cry unto the LORD our God for us, that he will save us out of the hand of the Philistines" (KJV). Israel was desperate. Luther said, "No one prays for anything deeply who has not been deeply alarmed." Again the centrality and absolute necessity of prayer surfaces. A recent poll revealed that the average pastor prays only nine minutes a day, the

average church member only three. Prayerless preachers produce powerless pulpits and problem pews, as Stephen Olford
put it. Leonard Ravenhill said the church was dead on its feet
because it was not living on its knees. But Samuel stood in the
breach and prayed. Thank God for the prophet-priest who
prays. But remember, in the New Testament sense, all God's
people are "priests" (1 Peter 2:5). Therefore, all believers are
called to stand in the gap and intercede for the land until the
awakening comes. Prayer is a vital ministry for every believer.
May it never be said of our day, God "wondered that there was
no intercessor" (Isaiah 59:16, KJV). May God raise up prayer
warriors!

The Concert of Prayer

As seen earlier, the First Great Awakening under Edwards
and Whitefield grew out of and was carried on through the
"Concert of Prayer."* Edwards wrote a classic book on the
theme of a "Concert of Prayer," entitling it, *An Humble Attempt
to Promote an Explicit Agreement and Visible Union of God's
People Through the World, in Extraordinary Prayer, for the Revival of Religion, and the Advancement of Christ's Kingdom on
Earth, Pursuant to Scripture-Promises and Prophecies Concerning the Last Time.* (That's the title, not the book.) Although
written many years ago, it still retains its relevance. Edwards
wrote:

> The great outward calamities in which the world is in-
> volved, and particularly the bloody war that embroils and
> wastes the nations . . . and in which our nation has so great
> a share, may well make all that believe God's word and love
> mankind, earnestly long and pray for that day when the
> wolf shall dwell with the lamb, and the nations shall beat
> their swords into plow-shares . . .
> But especially do the spiritual calamities and miseries
> of the present time, shew our great need of that blessed
> effusion of God's spirit. May not an attentive view and con-
> sideration of such a state of things well influence the people
> that favor the dust of Zion, to earnestness in their cries to

---

*This theme, mentioned often, will be taken up in detail in the Epilogue of this
book.

God for a general outpouring of his spirit, which alone can be an effectual remedy for these evils?[6]

That Spirit of prayer became instrumental in precipitating the Second Great Awakening. In the setting of that revival, early in the year of 1799, Rev. William F. Miller of Windsor, Connecticut, became deeply concerned about the spiritual conditions of the day. He called his church to a "Concert of Prayer." He reported:

> I appointed a weekly conference in the latter part of the month of February 1799, for this purpose, believing that the prevailing wickedness of the day called for extraordinary prayer to God. The appointment was successful far beyond what had been expected in bringing many people together to unite in prayer to God, and in seeking the precious blessings of His grace.[7]

In answer to the prayers of the people, God began to pour out His Spirit in the latter part of April. A significant revival broke and many people began to seek God. Those who sought, found life. History has repeatedly demonstrated that when people truly seek God, a revival is soon at hand. It has always been so. The prophet Isaiah fervently prayed:

> Oh that thou wouldest rend the heavens, that thou wouldest come down, that the mountains might flow down at thy presence, As when the melting fire burneth, the fire causeth the waters to boil, to make thy name known to thine adversaries, that the nations may tremble at thy presence! (Isaiah 64:1–2, KJV).

But where are the challenges to pray today? Andrew Murray said, "The man who calls the church to prayer will make the greatest contribution to world evangelization in history." Samuel the prophet realized the dire necessity of intercession. He cried out, "Gather all Israel at Mizpeh, and I will pray for you unto the LORD" (1 Samuel 7:5, KJV). Mizpeh means "Watchtower." Who will gather at the "watchtower" and pray, "Watchman, what of the night?" (Isaiah 21:11, KJV).

Sacrifice and Cleansing

Samuel first "poured out water before the LORD" and then "confessed their sins" (1 Samuel 7:6). The Targum translates this verse as "pouring out their hearts in repentance before the LORD." Now they are ready for the next sacrifice. "And Samuel took a sucking lamb, and offered it for a burnt offering wholly unto the LORD: and Samuel cried unto the LORD of Israel; and the LORD heard him" (1 Samuel 7:9, KJV). After their sin had been atoned for, forgiving love came in like a flood. God revived Israel. The Lord of love heard and "the land was healed."

> O, love of God,
> How rich and pure,
> How measureless and strong.
> It shall forevermore endure,
> The saints' and angels' song.

A beautiful healing epilogue emerges in the Samuel revival. After repentance, prayer, and forgiveness, the loving Lord led Israel out against their enemies. We can be sure that the devil will raise up enemies against God's revived people; the battle has no end. Actually, during revival, the warfare rages as never before. But God grants His people victory. "The LORD thundered with a great thunder on that day upon the Philistines, and discomfited them; and they were smitten before Israel" (1 Samuel 7:10b, KJV). The Lord routed the Philistines. When God speaks, *all* enemies flee. "We are more than conquerors through him that loved us" (Romans 8:37, KJV).

Then came the climax. "Samuel took a stone, and set it between Mizpeh and Shen, and called the name of it Ebenezer, saying, Hitherto hath the LORD helped us" (1 Samuel 7:12, KJV). "Ebenezer": the stone of help! Notice it is not just help, it is the *Lord's help*. God's *presence* had returned. The Glory shone forth over Israel again. The nation was reborn and, with God's power, the Philistines were subdued. Furthermore, "They came no more into the coast of Israel: and the hand of the LORD was against the Philistines all the days of Samuel" (1 Samuel 7:13, KJV). God's victories last.

Conclusion

Israel had journeyed in the Spirit all the way from "Ichabod" to "Ebenezer." Few question the necessity of the journey today. May the hour soon come when we can raise our united voice in praise and sing sincerely with Robert Robinson who wrote:

> Here I raise my Ebenezer;
> Hither by thy help I'm come;
> And I hope by thy good pleasure
> Safely to arrive at home.

Ichabod to Ebenezer! Healing of our land! It can happen, for "God is love."

A Wise Man's Wisest Move

In a Spiritual Awakening God Reveals Himself as

AVAILABLE

Therefore, "Pray."
2 CHRONICLES 6–7

Introduction

More has probably been written, preached, and taught concerning prayer than any other Christian discipline. Most believers readily realize that prayer stands as vital to spirituality and effectiveness in life and service. Not only that, God actually makes himself "available" in respect to our prayer. The centrality of intercession relative to instigating a spiritual awakening has been stressed almost to a fault. But still we do not pray, or at least we do not pray very much. Why?

No doubt a multitude of reasons can be raised as to why prayer seems so lacking in the lives of God's people today. In the first place, an intercessory prayer life demands discipline; that is never easy for anyone. Of the twelve Hebrew words used in the Old Testament that are translated "to pray," the one implied in our theme text actually means to "judge one's self habitually." Thus prayer in the biblical sense means consistent heart searching and continual repentance. That certainly has its price. Consequently, many "would-be" intercessors shy away. Then on the other hand, prayer often appears rather passive, and being the activists most of us are, we may find it difficult "just to pray." Further, intercession often produces no *immediate* results. Pragmatists have real problems here, and that means many of us. Not only that, prayer—especially prayer meetings—can actually seem boring. For an age caught up in religious excitement and entertainment, that too presents a problem. But the essential reason for prayerlessness probably centers in the fact that disciplined intercession involves stressful spiritual struggle and warfare. Hence, those accustomed to religious ease just cannot find strength to engage in the battle. The "flesh," so it seems, will do anything but pray. It remains everlastingly true, Satan fights furiously the interceding Christian. The old cliche has it right: The devil trembles when he sees the weakest saints upon their knees. The adversary will not make real prayer easy for anyone. And there are, no doubt, a thousand other reasons, or excuses, why many churches today have virtually become prayerless churches.

Our lack of prayer has exacted a tremendous toll. Spiritual immaturity, ministry ineptness, poverty of power—not to mention the strife, division, sin, and animosity in the churches—is the price we pay for our neglect of disciplined private and corporate prayer. And then add to all that the tragedies in society that come about as a consequence of the fact that the "salt has lost its savor." Above all, the church is failing to evangelize the world as it should, and that spells eternal tragedy. It sums itself up in the foundational reality that we are not experiencing revival today because we are not praying today. Our ark simply cannot weather the deluge of prayerlessness. It is as if we are starving to death; a feast is set before us, and for no real reason we refuse to eat. It really does not make sense.

But *if* we will pray, *if* we will get before God personally, *if* we will develop prayer groups, *if* church leaders will organize a vital prayer ministry in the churches, then God will surely show us His plan of prayer, make himself available, and make the exercise a vital means of producing spiritual awakening. God is far more ready to give than we are to receive.

Solomon's Prayer Revival

The beautiful pattern of intercession that brings revival is found in Solomon's prayer at the dedication of the temple. A more fitting passage for the concluding chapter of this plea for a spiritual awakening today can scarcely be found, and it fulfills that last word of the theme text of this book: "Pray." The theme text of this book itself, as evident, is cast in the context of Solomon's dedicatory prayer. Solomon was the world's wisest man. But the wisest move he ever made was to pray.

With all these truths in the background, we proceed to discover in detail how God honors intercessors and makes himself readily available for a spiritual awakening today. Effectual prayer for revival begins with a grasp of God's essential nature.

Understanding Who God Actually Is

Solomon knew the God to whom he prayed, and that knowledge formed the faith foundation of his effective intercession. When King Solomon realized who God is and what He does, that understanding gave him faith to address God in confidence. Actually, that basic principle of prayer is what this book has been all about. And although we have already looked at length at a number of God's great attributes in the previous chapters, an overview of those qualities of the mighty God whom Solomon presents in his dedicatory prayer may help us even more to pray the prayer of faith for revival.

God's Attributes: A Basis for Prayer

Solomon begins his intercessory prayer by reiterating the essential reality of God's nature: *His ultimacy.* "But will God dwell indeed with man on the earth? Behold, heaven and the highest heaven cannot contain thee; how much less this house which I have built!" (2 Chronicles 6:18, RSV). Solomon fully realized that the God he addressed was not a mere tribal deity of the Jews, certainly not anything like the Baals of the surrounding nations. Solomon's God invariably reveals himself as transcendently infinite and ultimate: the *only* true, creating God. He inhabits eternity, and stands before His universe utterly unlimited and immutable. He really does have the "whole world in His hand." After all, He created all things; therefore, He controls all reality as its Sovereign Ruler. The dictionary defines sovereignty as: "Supremacy of authority or rule, as exercised by a sovereign." That is our God. He rules all. As Job said, "I know that thou canst do all things, and that no purpose of thine can be thwarted" (Job 42:2, RSV). Nothing in all creation happens beyond His ultimate purpose and will. He accomplishes His purpose because He is sovereign. He rules because He is omnipotent. The theologians define omnipotence as "the power of God to do all things which are objects of power."[1] As the Bible says, "With God all things are possible" (Mark 10:27, KJV). Our God reigns.

The Fallacy of Process Theology

How woefully inadequate the contemporary concepts of the so-called "process theologians" appear in the biblical light of God's ultimacy. These theologians tell us that God himself moves along developmentally in "process," thus unable to cope fully at this stage with all of life's problems. They argue God may become infinite sometime in the future, but He has a developmental process to go through like all nature; that is to say, He is in "process." In the meantime, there are situations God cannot quite handle at this stage of His process. That hardly sounds like *ultimacy.*

Despite the popularity of process theology, these theologians project themselves into a very precarious position. They place themselves on shaky ground because, first of all, most of them grant that God is the Creator of all reality. But if their process presuppositions are true, then God has created an order of reality He **cannot** quite cope with, at least at this stage in time. The question then immediately rears up its stubborn head: How could God possibly create something greater or "stronger" than himself? Anything God cannot "handle"—even if at the temporary moment—surely stands as "stronger" or greater than He. That, of course, is nonsensical. How could *any* creator create *any* order greater than its own creator?

But, these thinkers may retort, there are certain situations God has created that by their very nature ascend above or at least rise parallel with God and thus He cannot quite cope with them, like the "inevitability" of evil and suffering. That line becomes an even worse admission as it precipitates on ultimate dualism: God and the inevitable situation. No serious Christian theologian or philosopher can abide an ultimate dualism. That virtually produces a polytheism. However, process thinkers state, God will one day conquer all foes, so it is not an *ultimate* dualism nor has God thus constructed something He will not be able to handle sometime in the future. Yet, that argument puts God on a finite time plane, and even the secular scientists know that time and space are finite and intertwined. So, if God created space—which process theologians admit—He also created time, and we are back to square one with God creating something "greater" than himself, that is, God is subject to the created "time process." Thus, He created a finite entity, a "time process," greater than himself, because according to process thought He is subject to it. Either that is true or the "time process" is an ultimate entity, and you are left once more with a dualism, not to mention the fact that we know scientifically that "time" is finite and relative. The basic presuppositions of the process thinkers are clearly untenable.

Moreover, if any entity is greater, or as great as, God, then that entity actually becomes God. And as if these thinkers argue that time and/or space are not *really* greater than God and only appear to be "at the moment," then God is playing games with us and just appears to be in process. It is very difficult to believe God engages in these sorts of games.

Of course, the argument put forward by process thinkers, to resolve their dilemma that God will one day become transcendent, actually puts the "process," that is leading God to transcendence, above God. And as if to save themselves from such contradictions or a dualism, they further argue that this "process" innately resides in the nature of God. That becomes tantamount to saying God is transcendent in the first place and thus can hardly be in "process." So we are back to God playing games.

Thus the entire process-theology scheme falls to the ground in a shambles of inner-contradictions, if not outright absurdities. How any thinking Christian, let alone a Bible-believing one, can embrace the process view of God remains a mystery. May this heresy perish.* The God of the Bible is ultimate, infinite, changeless, transcendent, and sovereign. As one commentator put it, "He is infinitely beyond the bounds of creation and infinitely above the praises of all intelligent creatures."[2] *He is Lord.*

Therefore, this God of ours can cope with anything. The tragic error of "process theology" is that it not only degrades God by putting Him on a process plane, but it also defuses the prayer of faith. How could a God who is still attempting to deal adequately with life's pressing issues be a God who inspires one to pray? I might find myself in a situation that God cannot

---

*This "new" theology is really not new. Edgar S. Brightman propounded the basic idea many years ago in his so-called "finite God" concept.

handle, so why pray. And to answer, "We never know so we should pray anyway just in case God can cope," hardly kindles my faith. *But God is infinite.* He can answer prayer, and prayer actually does change things. Intercession is not a mere psychological exercise on our part to get our spiritual psyche right—although that is a positive spin-off. Prayer changes *things.* Things take place through prayer that will not take place if we fail to pray. That stands as eternally true because God has all power and God has put His infinite power subject to our intercessory prayer of faith.

Here emerges a great mystery: an infinite, ultimate God who can do as He wishes, yet in certain areas of experience He subjects himself to our prayers. What a marvel! Without that foundational reality before us when we pray, the prayer of faith rarely gets prayed. And never are we to forget that to pray in faith is essential to receive answers. James said, "But let him ask in faith, with no doubting, for he who doubts is like a wave of the sea that is driven and tossed by the wind. For that person must not suppose that a double-minded man, unstable in all his ways, will receive anything from the Lord" (James 1:6–8, RSV).

God Is Holy

God, however, reveals himself as more than infinite, as foundational as that may be. Solomon also recognized God's essential nature as *holy.* We have seen in chapter four that this attribute of God stands as central to His very personhood. It warrants a few more words, especially in the light and context of prayer for spiritual awakening. Solomon prayed, "The LORD has said that he would dwell in thick darkness" (2 Chronicles 6:1, RSV). The metaphor "thick darkness" often speaks of the hidden holiness of God. The theme threads its way through much of the Bible. When Moses was on the holy mount, God appeared "wrapped in darkness, cloud, and gloom" (Deuteronomy 4:11, KJV). The vision of this holy God that Isaiah experienced came to the prophet as "the temple . . . filled with smoke" (Isaiah 6:4).

The Book of Hebrews tells us this obscuring of God by "clouds," "darkness," and "smoke" speaks of the "hiddenness" of God. But why "hidden"? Because He is utter holiness. And because we are the antithesis, sinful, God says, "You cannot see my face; for man shall not see me and live" (Exodus 33:20, RSV). God's naked holiness would consume us in an instant. So in grace He "hides" himself lest we be consumed. When the glorious day arrives that we actually fall before our God and see Him in fullness, then we will recognize that the one overwhelming attribute that prostrates us before the glory of His presence is His utter holiness.

What do we mean by the "holiness" of God? Theologian A. H. Strong says:

> Holiness is self-affirming purity. In virtue of this attribute of His nature, God eternally wills and maintains His own moral excellence. Moreover, all this shines forth as gloriously true of God and by revelation made evident and open to us several different ways:
> (a) From Scripture—"For it is written: 'Be holy, because I am holy' " (1 Peter 1:16).
> (b) From our own moral constitution—in which conscience asserts its supremacy over every other impulse and affection of our nature.
> (c) From the actual dealings of God—in which holiness conditions and limits the exercise of other attributes.
> (d) From God's eternal purpose of salvation—in which justice and mercy are reconciled only through the foreseen and predetermined sacrifice of Christ.[3]

Theologian Strong has hit the target; holiness finds its grounding in the very nature of God. Many Christians have seemingly assimilated such a sentimental view of God that it has precipitated a quiet, faulty Christian experience. To fail to understand the holiness of God, one can easily fall into the practical trap expressed by J. C. Ryle:

> There is an Athenian love of novelty abroad, and a morbid distaste for anything old and regular, and in the beaten path of our forefathers. Thousands will crowd to hear a new voice and a new doctrine, without considering for a moment whether what they hear is true. There is an incessant craving after any teaching which is sensational; and exciting, and rousing to the feelings. There is an unhealthy appetite for a sort of spasmodic and hysterical Christianity. The re-

ligious life of many is little better than spiritual dram-
drinking and the "meek and quiet spirit" which St. Peter
commends is clean forgotten (1 Peter 3:4). . . . If, in addition
to this, the true-hearted advocates of increased holiness are
going to fall out by the way and misunderstand one another,
it will be sadder still. We shall indeed be in evil plight.[4]

Ryle is right. Any diminution of the essential and fundamental holiness of God will inevitably precipitate a perverted
understanding of the holiness God demands in His people.
When that occurs, our grasp of Christian experience will degenerate into humanism, emotionalism, if not outright sensuality and worldliness. That will never produce effectual prayer
for revival, or prayer for anything else as far as that goes. God
always reveals himself as Holy in a spiritual awakening. That
is what lies back of Jesus' insistence that we pray "in [His]
name" (John 16:23–24). Because of the holiness of God and our
antithetical sinfulness, the only right we have to stand before
Him is because we can come in Jesus' name, that is, in His
righteousness and holiness. Our Savior alone makes us acceptable in God's holy presence, thus able to pray effectively. To
pray "in Jesus' name" is no mere pious platitude we pin on the
end of our prayers.

God Is Love

God is not only infinite holiness, which might imply He
resides transcendently far from us sinful creatures; Solomon
knew Him as a God of *steadfast love*. "God is love" (1 John 4:16).
The object of that divine love is humanity: you and me. Thus
Solomon prayed, "O LORD, God of Israel, there is no God like
thee, in heaven or on earth, keeping covenant and showing
steadfast love to thy servants who walk before thee with all
their heart" (2 Chronicles 6:14, RSV). Notice, His covenant of
love enables us to walk before Him. Although He is utterly holy
and dwells in "unapproachable light" (1 Timothy 6:16), if we
"walk in the light, as he is in the light, we have fellowship with
one another" (1 John 1:7). Through Jesus Christ, the transcendent God becomes the intimate loving Father. That gracious,
unchanging love forms the basis of our claim for answers to
prayer. He loves us, and love longs to give. That is the kind of

Father He is. Therefore, we can come to Him in perfect confidence because "perfect love drives out fear" (1 John 4:18). And because of all these magnificent attributes of God, He enters into a covenant relationship with us.

The Covenant Principle

God has always worked among and through His people on the basis of the "covenant of love." Adam lived in covenant with God in Eden (Genesis 1–2). Noah moved into covenant with God after the flood (Genesis 9:8–17); hence, the rainbow. God called Abraham into covenant relationship with himself as Abraham left Ur of the Chaldees (Genesis 12:1–2). The great covenant of the Law came thundering to Israel at the foot of Mount Sinai (Exodus 19–20). The greatest and most glorious of all the covenants, however, and the one to which all others pointed, is the New Covenant of grace in Christ Jesus (Hebrews 8:6–13).

The centrality of covenant in spiritual awakenings has been alluded to often. Now is the time to see what actually constitutes a covenant. Theologians define the term as, "A gracious undertaking entered into by God for the benefit and blessing of man, and specifically of those men who by faith receive the promises and commit themselves to the obligations which this undertaking involves."[5] The concepts contained in this definition are perfectly expressed in the covenants instituted by the grace of God. Several things need to be made clear about the love covenant principle. It will help our prayer life tremendously to realize all that resides in this marvelous truth.

First, the initiation for the establishment of the covenant of grace centers in God. God is the author of the covenant relationship. Then, the Holy Spirit actualizes it in human experience. The Spirit calls people to God (John 6:24; 16:7–11). In the New Covenant of Christ, the Spirit reveals the Lord Jesus (John 14:15). The Third Person of the Trinity then regenerates (John 3:5), and finally seals (Ephesians 1:13), sanctifies (Romans 15–16), and will one day raise up the believer in Christ (1 Thessalonians 4:15–18). To all these covenant blessings we have been predestined and called by God (Ephesians 1:3–10). Jesus Christ said, "You have not chosen me, but I have chosen you" (John 15:16, KJV). These are some of the glories of the love

197

covenant principle, *and God has done it all*. It is all of grace. Of course, a person must respond to God's covenant call. The invitation of God to His new covenant life must be accepted by repentance and faith. Therein we have another example of the scriptural paradox of divine election and human responsibility.

Therefore, when we respond to God's sovereign call and become a believer through repentance and faith (Acts 20:21), we enter into a loving grace covenant fellowship with the living God. Our gracious Lord has, in love, made us a covenant people, brought into dynamic relationship with our redeeming Savior to do His will, keep His covenant, and bring glory to His name.

All this means God, in steadfast, covenant love, will keep His promises concerning prayer for spiritual awakening. Solomon prayed, "Blessed be the LORD, the God of Israel, who with his hand has fulfilled what he promised with his mouth to David my father" (2 Chronicles 6:4, RSV). Because of His ultimacy, He can keep His Word. Because of His holiness, He will keep His Word for His name's sake. Because of His love, He keeps His Word for our good and His glory. Because of His covenant, He unfailingly keeps His Word. What an incentive to pray for an awakening. Space fails to list even a small portion of the promises of God concerning prayer for revival. But here is a beginning:

> Though I walk in the midst of trouble, thou wilt revive me; thou shalt stretch forth thine hand against the wrath of my enemies, and thy right hand shall save me (Psalm 138:7, KJV).

> For thus says the high and lofty One who inhabits eternity, whose name is Holy: "I dwell in the high and holy place, and also with him who is of a contrite and humble spirit, to revive the spirit of the humble, and to revive the heart of the contrite" (Isaiah 57:15, RSV).

> After two days he will revive us; on the third day he will raise us up, that we may live before him (Hosea 6:2, RSV).

> O LORD, I have heard the report of thee, and thy work, O LORD, do I fear. In the midst of the years renew it; in the midst of the years make it known; in wrath remember mercy (Habakkuk 3:2, RSV).

> But now for a brief moment favor has been shown by the LORD our God, to leave us a remnant, and to give us a secure hold within his holy place, that our God may

brighten our eyes and grant us a little reviving in our bondage. For we are bondmen; yet our God has not forsaken us in our bondage, but has extended to us his steadfast love before the kings of Persia, to grant us some reviving to set up the house of our God, to repair its ruins, and to give us protection in Judea and Jerusalem (Ezra 9:8–9, RSV).

But they who wait for the LORD shall renew their strength, they shall mount up with wings like eagles, they shall run and not be weary, they shall walk and not faint (Isaiah 40:31, RSV).

In one sense, Solomon said it all when he prayed,

Now, O my God, let thy eyes be open and thy ears attentive to a prayer of this place (2 Chronicles 6:40, RSV).

Solomon had absolute confidence in the fact that God hears and answers prayer. Furthermore, King Solomon realized that prayer, in its simplest form, is *asking*; and God's hearing is our *receiving*. That does not preclude praise, thanksgiving, or adoration, but praying is asking and God's hearing is receiving (1 John 5:14–15). He so loves to answer our prayers that He gives us His Holy Spirit to make our prayers acceptable in His sight:

Likewise the Spirit helps us in our weakness; for we do not know how to pray as we ought, but the Spirit himself intercedes for us with sighs too deep for words. And he who searches the hearts of men knows what is the mind of the Spirit, because the Spirit intercedes for the saints according to the will of God (Romans 8:26–27, RSV).

Take heart, God will hear the revival cry: "Wilt thou not revive us again" (Psalm 85:6).

God's Honor

The final divine attribute Solomon rests upon, as he lifts his voice to God, centers in the reality that God will surely *honor and glorify His Name*. To glorify himself is part of God's intrinsic nature. God himself set His Name on the temple, and that holy Name He will surely magnify:

Since the day that I brought my people out of the land

of Egypt, I chose no city in all the tribes of Israel in which to build a house, that my name might be there (2 Chronicles 6:5, RSV).

The scriptural use of the word "Name," as it relates to Yahweh, always speaks of the very essence and nature of God. Thus, when God says He will honor His Name, He is really saying He will honor himself and all that He is. The New Testament reveals the same emphasis. For example, Philippians 2:10–11 reads: "That at the name of Jesus every knee should bow, in heaven and on earth and under the earth, and every tongue confess that Jesus Christ is Lord, to the glory of God the Father" (RSV). In the end, the entire universe shall be a glory to God and His infinite, holy, loving, covenant grace.

Now if all this be true concerning the kind of God we address in prayer for spiritual awakening, how can we ever doubt that He will "hear from heaven, forgive our sin, and heal our land"? Everything God is assures answered prayer. He reveals himself as "available" to us when we cry to Him. Therefore, rest in His reality and pray.

But that raises the next logical question: Exactly *what* should we pray for as we begin interceding for a fresh touch from God? Solomon's prayer presents those principles as well.

Prayer's Objectives in Spiritual Awakening

As has been emphasized almost endless times, before revival comes, God first deals with sin. Therefore, all effective revival praying begins there. Solomon said,

> If they sin against thee—for there is no man who does not sin—and thou art angry with them, and dost give them to an enemy, so that they are carried away captive to a land far or near . . . then hear thou from heaven thy dwelling place their prayer and their supplications, and maintain their cause and forgive thy people who have sinned against thee (2 Chronicles 6:36, 39, RSV).

So much has been related on this theme, few words are needed here. Only once more let it be said: If there is no cleansing, there will be no filling. If there is no confession, there will be no blessing. Revival waits on the "break up of unplowed ground" (Jeremiah 4:3).

Hard on the heels of broken confession of sin comes the plea for forgiveness: "And hearken thou to the supplications of thy servant and of thy people Israel, when they pray toward this place; yea, hear thou from heaven thy dwelling place; and when thou hearest, forgive" (2 Chronicles 6:21, RSV). To ask for forgiveness as we confess our sins is a most natural exercise. Some say that believers should never actually ask for forgiveness, all we need to do is confess our sins. They argue 1 John 1:9 states no more than: "If we confess our sins, he is faithful and just, and will forgive our sins and cleanse us from all unrighteousness." But that is probably splitting theological hairs too finely. When we brokenheartedly confess our sins, we just naturally ask for forgiveness. And, after all, Jesus taught us to pray, "Forgive us our debts, as we also have forgiven our debtors" (Matthew 6:12). Simply put, seeking revival means seeking forgiveness and cleansing.

The Outward Look

Then the tenor of Solomon's prayer changed—as should ours. After the "journey inward," a "journey outward" becomes mandatory. Revival never ends in introspection and personal inward existential experience, although it surely begins there. Some have gotten hung up on that exercise. There must be the outward look, and hence outgoing prayer. Thus, Solomon prayed, "Then hear thou from heaven, and act, and judge thy servants, requiting the guilty by bringing his conduct upon his own head, and vindicating the righteous by rewarding him according to his righteousness" (2 Chronicles 6:23, RSV). The king prayed for the vindication of God's righteousness. Justice must prevail in the church and in society if either is to stand. For that we ought to pray. And, as previously pointed out, there has never been a true awakening where there was not a giant step forward in spiritual justice and social righteousness.

We are to pray for the defeat of evil. But that means *real warfare.* Solomon realized this fact. The Jews as a nation had been defeated time and time again. The devil had often devastated their land. So the king prayed: "Then hear thou from heaven, and forgive the sin of thy people Israel, and bring them again to the land which thou gavest to them and to their fathers" (2 Chronicles 6:25, RSV). Solomon's prayer sought to regain lost land. It is so easy to lose that which we had once gained. Paul wrote, "Only let us hold true to what we have attained" (Philippians 3:16, RSV).

The fact that many churches are losing ground today is obvious. Great churches, former lighthouses of the Gospel, are letting cities slip through their fingers as their light grows dim. The fog of apathy that swirls around us seems at times almost to engulf us, extinguishing the light completely. Consequently, we tend to retreat to what appears to give some reprieve. And how strange are the refuges to *where* we often retreat. Some scurry into theological deviations of the orthodox Gospel to justify the deterioration. Others give themselves to some form of institutionalism and formalism and derive their satisfaction in those realms of irrelevancy. Some entrench themselves in cold orthodoxy, thinking as long as they are orthodox on every minute point of doctrine they are secure. Many retreat into an esoteric, emotional religious ghetto, and thus never really face the problems. There are those who simply settle down to a "maintenance ministry" and hope for better days—but they never come. Must we lose ground? Are Satan's entrenchments and onslaughts invincible? Must we go on like this? Never! Revival can come, and when it does, we will not only regain what we have lost, new land will be conquered. We can be like the Israelites when they finally got out of the wilderness; they crossed the Jordan and the walls of Jericho came falling down and they went forth as the conquering people of God. To that end we should battle. But we must remember, as Paul put it, "The weapons of our warfare are not carnal, but *mighty through God* to the pulling down of strong holds" (2 Corinthians 10:4, KJV). Satan and his host of demons who would pressure, possess, and pervert people can never be defeated with carnal weapons, that is, politics, manipulations, programs, and the like. People are not the enemy, the devil is the foe. We are in a spiritual battle, and it therefore takes spiritual weapons to win. The greatest of those weapons is obviously prayer. Intercession always stands as the great "overcomer" in spiritual warfare. Although Satan would put all his forces to defeat us, victory can be ours, *if we will pray.*

What a refreshment revival times are, when evil suffers an ignoble defeat. As Solomon prayed: "Then hear thou in heaven, and forgive the sin of thy servants, thy people Israel, when thou dost teach them the good way in which they should walk; and grant rain upon thy land, which thou hast given to thy people as an inheritance" (2 Chronicles 6:27, RSV). God grants "rain." The psalmist prayed a similar prayer: "Yea, the LORD will give what is good, and our land will yield its increase" (Psalm 85:12, RSV). God will "heal our land" (2 Chronicles 7:14) as the theme text of this volume promises. His grace and mercy extends itself limitlessly. As one commentator clearly expressed it: "And to what length does divine mercy go? Judaism insisted, 'To the limit of human imagination and beyond' . . . Christianity answered, 'Even to the Cross.' "[6]

Solomon prayed on, teaching us what to pray for in our revival intercessions:

> Likewise when a foreigner, who is not of thy people Israel, comes from a far country for the sake of thy great name, and thy mighty hand, and thy outstretched arm, when he comes and prays toward this house, hear thou from heaven thy dwelling place, and do according to all for which the foreigner calls to thee; in order that all the peoples of the earth may know thy name and fear thee, as do thy people Israel, and that they may know that this house which I have built is called by thy name (2 Chronicles 6:32–33, RSV).

Evangelization

Here we get to the real heart of God's purpose in awakening His people: the evangelizing of the "foreigner." We professing Christians must never forget we too were once "separated from Christ, alienated from the commonwealth of Israel, and strangers to the covenants of promise" (Ephesians 2:12, RSV). We were "foreigners." Then, by the infinite mercy of God, someone came along and pointed us to Christ and we were saved by His free grace through faith. That action expresses God's heart. It is the Father's will that none should perish, "but that all should come to repentance" (2 Peter 3:9, KJV). Let it be repeated over and over, any revival that does not result in fervent, effective, widespread evangelism has not accomplished what God desires. Somewhere the movement got sidetracked. And that is not to mention all the far-reaching social benefits that attend an awakening.

God's Exaltation

Finally, and ultimately, we pray that God's holy name may be exalted. Solomon expressed it correctly:

> And now arise, O LORD God, and go to thy resting place, thou and the ark of thy might. Let thy priests, O LORD God, be clothed with salvation, and let thy saints rejoice in thy goodness. O LORD God, do not turn away thy face of thy anointed one! Remember thy steadfast love for David thy servant (2 Chronicles 6:41–42, RSV).

Notice how the king phrased his prayer for God's glory; he asked that God might take His rightful place, and as a consequence, God's leaders will be clothed with salvation and the saints will rejoice in goodness. Salvation and goodness are what bring glory to God. When people enter into the salvation and goodness of God, His righteous name will be glorified. We must never forget that the chief end of life is to glorify God.

The Answer to Prayer

Did God answer Solomon's prayer? Chapter seven of 2 Chronicles tells us in graphic terms. First, the fire fell from heaven: "When Solomon had ended his prayer, fire came down from heaven and consumed the burnt offering and the sacrifices, and the glory of the LORD filled the temple" (2 Chronicles 7:1, RSV). Notice, the fire fell from heaven; it was not stoked up on earth. On Pentecost there came "a sound *from heaven*" and then the "tongues of fire . . . separated and came to rest on each of them" (Acts 2:3). Real revival falls from "above." And when the fire falls, unbelievable things occur.

As Solomon prayed, the fire of God's glory fell and filled the magnificent new temple, consuming the burnt offering he had laid before God. That dramatic sight meant God had accepted his sacrifice. That too always transpires when revival fires burn. This gracious God accepts our sacrifice of prayer, and thereby glorifies himself.

Praying Hyde

A moving illustration of the sacrifice and subsequent glory of revival prayer is exemplified in the life of missionary John Hyde. John finished his education at the McCormick Theological Seminary in Chicago, Illinois. Upon graduation he made his way to the West Coast and boarded a boat bound for India. He had dedicated his life to the mission field. As he embarked on the ship someone handed him a letter. In his stateroom he tore it open. It was a bon voyage letter from an old preacher friend.

But as Hyde eagerly opened the letter, he read a rather strange message: "Dear John, Are you filled with the Spirit?" That did not set too well with the young missionary. "Imagine," he said to himself, "that old preacher asking that. Why, I'm going to the mission field. What sort of a question is that?" In a fit of disturbed anger he crumpled up the letter, flung it on the stateroom floor, and paced out on the deck—and paced, and paced, and paced. God's convicting barb had pierced his proud young heart deeply, and there was no extricating of it. Finally, God broke John's heart. When he stepped off the ship on India's coral sands, he disembarked a different young man than what he was when he had boarded it in America.

Through the years of missionary service God gave John Hyde a most unusual missionary ministry: The Holy Spirit made a profound prayer warrior out of him. Through the years of missionary service, John's prayer life deepened until he was actually agonizing and praying four full hours each day. And it is not incidental that God also granted him four Indians won to Christ each day as well.

As time passed, Hyde became quite ill. A full physical examination was given. The physician said, "Mr. Hyde, what are you doing to yourself? What unusual stress, strain, and agony are you submitting to? Your physical heart is in the worst condition I have ever seen, it has actually moved in your chest cavity. What are you doing?"

When the great intercessor died, the eulogies that arose in

India were not to John Hyde, his name, but to *Praying Hyde*, the name by which the Indians knew and loved him, because he had moved their nation God-ward on his knees. A profound spiritual awakening emerged out of his sacrificial intercession. Yet, this is the sort of sacrifice that God accepts and through which He sends revival blessings.

Then we read in 2 Chronicles 7:1, "The glory of the LORD filled the temple." That inevitably happens when people pray for revival and God rends the heavens. Through Solomon's prayer, the glory of the Lord fell in such consuming holiness that the priest could not enter the temple (2 Chronicles 7:2). That is what we should pray for and that is what God longs to do. He is available.

The Results of Revival

The final results of revival praying are stated as follows: "When all the children of Israel saw the fire come down and the glory of the LORD upon the temple, they bowed down with their faces to the earth on the pavement, and worshiped and gave thanks to the LORD, saying, 'For he is good, for his steadfast love endures for ever' " (2 Chronicles 7:3, RSV). Humility and gratitude abounded. True worship emerged. The days of formality and superficiality ended. Not only that, God so manifested himself that the whole land learned of who He was: a God whose "steadfast love endures forever." That is revival.

Conclusion

So the issue becomes, will we pray for a spiritual awakening? Will we make the sacrifice, pay the price, and intercede until the fire falls? If we can become a true intercessor, great days are ahead, because God stands available for revival; therefore, *pray*.

To aid us in that ministry of intercession—prayer is certainly a ministry—we turn to a brief and final word in the Epilogue.

Creating a New Concert of Prayer for Spiritual Awakening

Beyond doubt, the greatest revival in the world today is occurring in South Korea, epitomized in the congregation in Seoul led by David Y. Cho. That great parable church has become symbolic of the tremendous movement.* All wonder at the multitudes they reach for Christ. What constitutes their secret? Pastor Cho himself tells us:

> In 1983 we had a total of one hundred twenty thousand new converts. Why are so many people being saved within a single church? We have seen the importance of developing and keeping a prayer life. If we stop praying, the revival will wane. If we continue praying, I believe that all Korea can be saved.
> I believe that the same level of revival can be experienced in your church. There is no land too hard for the Holy Spirit to work. There is no church too dead. There is no country too closed to the gospel. The answer is prayer![1]

What sort of person of prayer does it take to intercede for revival? What are the qualities of a revival intercessor? Cho states:

> Simeon, the man in the temple who saw the little child Jesus (Luke 2:25–35), is a perfect example of the qualities an intercessor should possess:
> 1. *He was devout!* A person who enters the ministry of intercession must be devoutly given to prayer.
> 2. *He was patient!* The Scripture says that Simeon waited

---

*Also noteworthy is the fact that the largest Methodist Church, Baptist Church, and Presbyterian Church in the world are in Seoul. All denominations are leaping forward in growth and ministry.

for the "Consolation of Israel." While most people were looking for a political solution, Simeon knew that Israel's solution was spiritual. Therefore, he could wait many years before seeing the results of his prayers.

3. *He was full of the Holy Spirit!* Only a man who has the Holy Spirit upon him can carry the weight of intercessory prayer.

4. *He trusted!* It had been revealed to Simeon that he would see the results of his prayer before death. Therefore, he went faithfully to the temple daily for many years until the day came when Christ was brought to the temple.

5. *He was a man of vision!* Simeon's prophecy over the Christ child brought marvel to Joseph and Mary. Therefore, he saw more about Christ than His natural mother and stepfather.[2]

May God raise up people of vision like Spirit-filled Simeon, willing to learn, wait, and become revival intercessors. One need not be already fully instructed in prayer to begin interceding, all it takes is willingness and discipline. And surely, there are at least some in all our churches who would be willing to learn and band themselves together to form a Concert of Prayer for a new spiritual awakening. They need not be many, for as we have seen several times, the Concert of Prayer of the few spawned many revivals.

The challenge to contemporary Christianity is tremendous. Division and apathy characterize too many churches, especially in America and Europe. Further, the problems of society in general are enormous. Crime is a deepening problem in the cities, the suburbs, and the small towns. Increasing numbers of people are homeless and destitute. Alcoholism, drug addiction, and mental illness affect large numbers. Social injustices abound on every hand. Many elderly people are lonely and neglected. People living on the streets increase daily. Forces destroying the moral fiber of young and old alike abound. People are frightened by the appearance of new sexually transmitted diseases. Hunger is everywhere. Sin that once was abhorrent to people is now accepted, even defended. And if a voice is raised, the protestor is labeled a bigot and ridiculed. In many respects society is humanistic, utterly secular if not anti-Christian. Thus it suffers the consequences of its weak and crumbling moral structures. Such a culture simply cannot stand.

This we know so well, and church programs often fail to meet the real needs of society. Thus, evangelism, missions, and effective ministry go wanting and the world sinks in the morass of final obliteration.

The Hope

Yet, in spite of all these perplexities, there are many who believe that the church stands on the edge of another Great Awakening that will reverse the entire headlong plunge to destruction. If such is the case, a renewed Concert of Prayer will be what brings it about. Will you therefore pray for renewal? Will you seek God to shower down a worldwide spiritual awakening in order that the task of world evangelization can be completed and the terrible erosion of society stopped? Will you stand in the gap? It is really the *only hope*. That is not the word of an alarmist, but a realist.

But we must pray according to God's plan as revealed in the Scriptures. David Y. Cho of Korea can help us again here. He presents four principles of prayer for spiritual awakening.

1. *We must ask in faith!* Simply asking God for things will not assure you of a positive response. "And all things, whatsoever ye shall ask in prayer, believing, ye shall receive" (Matthew 21:22).

2. *We must abide in a relationship with Christ!* "If ye abide in me, and my words abide in you, ye shall ask what ye will, and it shall be done unto you" (John 15:7, KJV). When we abide in prayer, we develop spiritually so that His desires are ours; therefore, this spiritual blank check can be entrusted to us.

3. *We must be motivated properly!* "When you ask, you do not receive, because you ask with wrong motives, that you may spend what you get on your pleasures" (James 4:3). It is God's desire to give us all good things; we know that. Yet, so many requests are generated by sheer selfishness. God desires that what we ask should be to the end that He may be glorified.

4. *We must ask in accordance with the will of God!* Does this mean that we should wonder whether God wants us healed before we pray for healing? No! This is why knowledge of Scripture is so important. The Bible tells

us what the will of God is. So, when we ask for something that God has promised us, then we know with certainty that we are praying in God's will: "This is the confidence we have in approaching God: that if we ask anything according to his will, he hears us. And if we know that he hears us—whatever we ask—we know that we have what we asked of him" (1 John 5:14–15).[3]

Further, we must develop a *plan* for a Concert of Prayer.

The Plan for a Concert of Prayer

I recommend that days of prayer, even fasting, be observed in the homes and churches of all concerned believers. These special days of prayer should involve private and corporate confession of sin and earnest prayer for an outpouring of God's Spirit to bring about the healing of the churches, homes, and society.

In addition, the churches should do all they can to encourage and nurture prayer groups within their congregations, neighborhoods, workplaces, homes, institutions, and on college and university campuses in their localities. Pastors and seminarians ought to give themselves to intercession. Some churches have developed a ministry of prayer that goes on in a "chain of prayer" for hours every day of the week. Prayer partners can be organized. Prayer breakfasts for men and prayer teas for women ought to be regularly scheduled. Moreover, sermons, seminars, conferences, and retreats devoted to prayer for spiritual awakening could do much to promote prayer for the interests of the church and the kingdom. Organization, education, inspiration, and above all prayer itself will be required to see the widespread proliferation of Concerts of Prayer. Every conceivable means of getting people to pray should be implemented. As we have repeatedly seen in this book, the Bible and subsequent history of spiritual awakenings has demonstrated incontestably that the Spirit of prayer is often poured out upon God's people as a massive prayer effort is mobilized. We are wise not to forget Matthew Henry's word: "When God is about to pour out unusual mercies on His people, He first of all sets them a-praying."

John Sutcliff, one of the founders of the Baptist Missionary

Society of England, expressed in 1789 the vision for the Concert of Prayer. These words are as relevant to our scene as if written today. He said:

> O for thousands upon thousands, divided into small bands in their respective cities, towns, villages, all met at the same time, and in pursuit of one end, offering up their united prayers, like so many ascending clouds of incense before the Most High! May He shower down blessings on all the scattered tribes of Zion!

Therefore, again we ask, will you pray? Will you call your church, group, and Christian friends to prayer? Will you start a Concert of Prayer in your circle? Will you specify a day and prepare to set people praying for spiritual awakening? Will you do something to get people to pray? Great times are ahead if we will. May we join the psalmist, and once more cry out to the God of revival, "Wilt thou not revive us again: that thy people may rejoice in thee? Shew us thy mercy, O LORD, and grant us thy salvation" (Psalm 85:6–7). For it is really true: "IF MY PEOPLE . . . WILL . . . THEN I WILL."

ENDNOTES

Prologue

1. Eric W. Hayden, *Spurgeon on Revival* (Grand Rapids: Zondervan Publishing House, 1962), p. 12.
2. Ibid., p. 57.
3. J. I. Parker, *Keep in Step With the Spirit* (Old Tappan, N.J.: Fleming H. Revell Co., 1984), pp. 225–258.

Chapter One

1. Mendell Taylor, *Exploring Evangelism* (Kansas City: Beacon Hill Press, 1964), p. 252.
2. Ibid., p. 254.
3. Walter C. Kaiser, Jr., *Quest for Revival* (Chicago: Moody Press, 1986), p. 118.
4. Bertha Smith, *Go Home and Tell* (Nashville: Broadman Press, 1965), pp. 14–17.
5. Burns, *Revivals: Their Laws and Leaders*, pp. 138–139.
6. C. E. Autrey, *Revivals of the Old Testament* (Grand Rapids: Zondervan Publishing House, 1960), p. 137.

Chapter Two

1. Taylor, *Exploring Evangelism*, p. 412.
2. *Connecticut Evangelical Magazine* V, September 1804.
3. Arthur W. Pink, *Gleanings in Exodus* (Chicago: Moody Press, 1964), p. 30.
4. Hayden, *Spurgeon on Revival*, p. 58.
5. Charles G. Finney, *Lectures on Revivals of Religion* (New York: Fleming H. Revell Company, 1868), p. 23.
6. Ibid., p. 26.
7. Ibid., p. 27.
8. Ibid., p. 27.
9. Ibid., p. 23.

Chapter Three

1. Burns, *Revivals: Their Laws and Leaders*, p. 287.
2. Ibid., p. 287.

3. Walter C. Kaiser, Jr., *Quest for Revival*, p. 99.
4. Arthur Fawcett, *The Cambuslang Revival* (London: The Banner of Truth Trust, 1971), p. 55.
5. Ibid., p. 112.
6. Ibid., p. 114.
7. Ibid., p. 115.
8. Ibid., p. 122.
9. Ibid., pp. 122–123.
10. F. W. Berume, *Billy Bray, The King's Son* (London: Epworth Press, 1877), p. 40.
11. Autrey, *Revivals in the Old Testament*, p. 119.
12. From an unpublished Ph.D. Thesis by Edward Charles Lyrene, Jr., *The Role of Prayer in American Revival Movements, 1740–1860*, (Louisville, KY.: The Southern Baptist Theological Seminary, 1985.)

Chapter Four

1. Charles H. Spurgeon, *The Treasury of the Bible*, N.T. Vol. 3 (Grand Rapids: Zondervan Publishing House, 1962), p. 29.
2. *The Broadman Bible Commentary*, Vol. 1 (Nashville: Broadman Press, 1969), p. 450.
3. Michael Green, *Evangelism in the Early Church* (London: Hodder and Stoughton, 1970), p. 249.
4. Edward C. Lyrene, Unpublished Ph.D. Thesis.
5. Arthur W. Pink, *Gleanings in Exodus* (Chicago: Moody Press, 1964), p. 323.
6. Walter C. Kaiser, Jr., *Quest for Revival*, p. 39.

Chapter Five

1. *Connecticut Evangelical Magazine* II, October 1801.

Chapter Six

1. G. Campbell Morgan, *The Acts of the Apostles* (London: Pickering and Ingles, Ltd., 1924), p. 12.
2. William Barclay, *The Acts of the Apostles* (Philadelphia: The Westminster Press, 1953), p. xiii.
3. Ibid., p. 5.
4. Stephen F. Olford, *Lord, Open the Heavens* (Wheaton: Harold Shaw Publishers, 1962), p. 60.
5. Charles G. Finney, *Memoirs* (New York: Fleming H. Revell Company, 1876), p. 103.
6. Charles G. Finney, *Power From on High* (Eastbourne: Essex, Victory Press, 1944), p. 9.

Chapter Seven

1. From a film produced by Campus Crusade International entitled *Prayer for Spiritual Awakening* by J. Edwin Orr.

2. Walter C. Kaiser, Jr., *Quest for Revival*. p. 54.
3. Alexander Maclaren, *Exposition of the Holy Scripture*, Vol. 2 (Grand Rapids: Eerdmans Publishing Company, 1944), p. 277.
4. Jonathan Goforth, *By My Spirit* (Minneapolis: Bethany House Publishers, 1942), pp. 21–22.
5. Ibid., p. 30.
6. Jonathan Edwards, *An Humble Attempt*, in Apocalyptic Writing, Vol. 5, ed. Stephen Stein (New Haven: Yale University Press, 1977).
7. *Connecticut Evangelical Magazine* I, January 1801, p. 269.

Chapter Eight

1. A. H. Strong, *Systematic Theology* (Philadelphia: The Judson Press, 1907), p. 286.
2. Matthew Henry, *Matthew Henry's Commentary on the Whole Bible*, Vol. II (New York: Fleming H. Revell Co.), p. 929.
3. Strong, *Systematic Theology*, pp. 268, 296–298.
4. J. C. Ryle, *Holiness* (London: James Clark and Co., Ltd., 1956), p. XVII.
5. *Baker's Dictionary of Theology* (Grand Rapids: Baker Book House, 1960), p. 142.
6. George Arthur Buttrick, Ed., *The Interpreter's Bible*, Vol. III (Nashville: Abindgon Press, 1954), p. 459.

Epilogue

1. Paul Y. Cho, *Prayer: Key to Revival* (Waco: Word Books, 1984), p. 20. (Pastor Cho has changed his name from Paul to David since the writing of his book on prayer.)
2. Ibid., p. 81.
3. Ibid., pp. 67–68.

SELECTED BIBLIOGRAPHY

Books on History and Principles of Spiritual Awakening, Prayer, and Personal Revival

Beardsley, Ph.d., S.T.D., Frank Grenville. *Religious Progress Through Religious Revivals.* American Tract Society, 1943.

Boles, John B., *The Great Revival 1787–1805.* Lexington: University of Kentucky Press, 1972.

Burns, James. *Revivals, Their Laws and Leaders.* Grand Rapids: Baker Book House, 1960.

Cairns, Earle E. *An Endless Line of Splendor.* Wheaton: Tyndale House Publishers, 1986.

Carwardine, Richard. *Trans-Atlantic Revivalisms.* Westport: Greenwood Press, 1978.

Chandler, D. D., LL. D., Warren A. *Great Revivals and the Great Republic.* Nashville: Tenn.: Dallas, Tex.: Publishing House of the M. E. Church, South Smith and Lamar, Agents, 1904.

Chappell, Frederic Leonard. *The Great Awakening of 1740.* American Baptist Publishing Society, 1903.

Cleveland, Catherine Caroline. *The Great Revival in the West.* Chicago: The University of Chicago Press, 1916.

Coleman, Robert Emerson. *One Divine Moment—The Asbury Revival.* Old Tappan, N. J.: Revell, 1970.

Cross, Whitney R. *The Burned-Over District.* New York: Harper and Row, 1950.

Culpepper, Charles. *The Shantung Revival.* Available at Mid-America Theological Seminary, Memphis, Tenn.

Drummond, Lewis A. *The Awakening That Must Come.* Nashville: Broadman Press, 1978.

——. *Charles Grandison Finney and the Birth of Modern Evangelism.* Minneapolis: Bethany Press, 1985.

——. *The Revived Life.* Nashville: Broadman Press, 1982.

——. *Spurgeon: Prince of Preachers.* Grand Rapids: Kregel Press, 1992.

Edwards, Brian H. *Revival: A People Saturated with God.* Durham: England: Evangelical Press, 1990.

Edwards, Jonathan. *The Narrative.* Grand Rapids: Kregel Publications, 1952.

Evans, Eifron. *Revival Comes to Wales,* and *The Welsh Revival of 1904.* Wales: The Evangelical Press of Wales, 1959 and 1969.

Evans, W. Glyn. *Profiles of Revival Leaders.* Nashville: Broadman Press, 1976.

Fawcett, Arthur. *The Cambuslang Revival.* London: The Banner of Truth Trust, 1971.

Finney, Charles G. *Memoirs.* New York: Revell, 1876.

————. *Lectures on Revivals of Religion.* New York: Revell, 1868.

Fish, H. C. *Handbook of Revivals.* Harrisonburg: Gano Books, 1874.

Gillies, John. *Accounts of Revival.* London: Banner of Truth Trust, 1981.

Goforth, Jonathan. *By My Spirit.* Minneapolis: Bethany House Publishers Publishers, 1942.

Harrison, Archibald W. *The Evangelical Revival and Christian Reunion.* The Epworth Press, 1942.

Hoffman, Fred W. *Revival Times in America.* Boston: W. Av Wilde Company, Boston, 1956.

Jones, S. Williams. *Christ in the Camp,* Harrisonburg: Sprinkle Publication, 1887.

Lacy, Jr., Benjamin Rice. *Revivals in the Midst of the Years.* Royal Publishers, Inc., 1968.

Lloyd-Jones, Martyn. *Revival.* Westchester: Crossway Books, 1987.

Miller, Percy. *The Great Awakening.* Indianapolis: Bobbs-Merrell Publishing Co., 1967.

Orr, Jr. Edwin. *The Eager Feet.* Chicago: Moody Press, 1975.

————. *The Flaming Tongue.* Chicago: Moody Press, 1973.

————. *The Second Evangelical Awakening in America.*

Scharpff, Paulus. *History of Evangelism.* Grand Rapids: Eerdman's, 1966.

Smith, Bertha. *Go Home and Tell.* Nashville: Broadman Press, 1965.

Smith, Timothy L. *Revivalism and Social Reform in Mid-Nineteenth-Century America.* New York/Nashville: Abingdon Press, 1957.

Sprague, William B. *Lectures on Revivals of Religion.* London: Banner of Truth Trust, 1959.

Stone, Barton. *The Cane Ridge Reader.* Cincinnati: J. A. James, 1847.

Thornburg, J. F. *God Sent Revival.* Grand Rapids: Evangelical Press, 1977.

Prayer and Personal Revival Books

Allen, Charles L. *All Things Are Possible Through Prayer.* Old Tappan: N. J.: Revell, 1958.

Appelman, Hyman. *Formula for Revival.*

Billheimer, Paul E. *Destined for the Throne.* Minneapolis: Bethany House Publishers, with Christian Literature Crusade, 1975.

Bisagno, John. *The Power of Positive Praying.* Grand Rapids: Zondervan, 1965.

Blaiklock, E. M. *The Positive Power of Prayer.* Glendale, Calif.: Regal, 1974.

Blessitt, Arthur. *Tell the World—A Jesus People Manual.* Old Tappan, N. J.: Revell, 1969.

Bounds, E. M. *The Essentials of Prayer.* Minneapolis: Bethany House Publishers, 1976.

———. *The Necessity of Prayer.* Grand Rapids: Baker Book House, 1976.

———. *The Possibilities of Prayer.* Grand Rapids: Baker Book House, 1978.

———. *Power Through Prayer.* London: Marshall, n.d.

———. *Prayer and Praying Men.* Grand Rapids: Baker Book House, 1977.

———. *Purpose in Prayer.* Grand Rapids: Baker Book House, 1978.

———. *The Reality of Prayer.* Grand Rapids: Baker Book House, 1978.

———. *A Treasury of Prayer.* Minneapolis: Bethany House Publishers, 1961. (Compiled by Leonard Ravenhill.)

———. *The Weapon of Prayer.* Grand Rapids: Baker Book House, 1975.

Bunyan, John. *Prayer.* London: Banner of Truth Trust, 1965.

Chadwick, Samuel. *The Path of Prayer.* Fort Washington, Penn.: Christian Literature Crusade, 1963.

Cho, Paul Y. *Prayer: Key to Revival.* Waco, Tex.: Word Books, 1984.

Christenson, Evelyn, and Viola Blake. *What Happens When Women Pray.* Wheaton, Ill.: Victor Books, 1976.

Coleman, Robert Emerson. *Dry Bones Can Live Again.* Old Tappan, N. J.: Revell, 1969.

Demaray, Donald E. *Alive to God Through Prayer.* Grand Rapids: Baker Book House, 1965.

Eastman, Dick. *No Easy Road.* Grand Rapids: Baker Book House, 1971.

———. *The Hour that Changes the World.* Grand Rapids: Baker Book House, 1978.

Edwards, Jonathan. *The Life of Reverend David Brainerd.* Grand Rapids: Baker Book House, 1978.

Emerick, ———. *A Manual for Prayer.* Nashville: The Upper Room, 1958.

Findlay, James F. *Dwight L. Moody.* Chicago: University of Chicago Press, 1969.

Finney, Charles G. *Prevailing Prayer.* Grand Rapids: Kregel, 1965.

Fischer, H. A. *Reviving Revivals.*

Gesswein, Armin R. *Seven Wonders of Prayer.* Grand Rapids: Zondervan, 1957.

Goestsch, Ronald W. *Power Through Prayer.* St. Louis, Mo.: Concordia Publishing House, 1959.

Goforth, Rosalind. *How I Know God Answers Prayer.* New York: Grosset and Dunlap, 1904.

Grubb, Norman. *Continuous Revival.* Fort Washington, Penn.: Christian Literature Crusade, 1961–63.

————. *Rees Howells: Intercessor.* Fort Washington, Penn.: Christian Literature Crusade, 1962.

Hallesby, O. *Prayer.* Minneapolis: Augsburg Publishing House, 1959.

Hanne, John Anthony. *Prayer or Pretense?* Grand Rapids: Zondervan, 1974.

Harvey, Edwin and Lillian. *Kneeling We Triumph.* Chicago: Moody Press, 1974.

Hasler, Richard. *Journey with David Brainerd.* Downers Grove, Ill.: InterVarsity Press, 1976.

Hayford, Jack W. *Prayer Is Invading the Impossible.* Plainfield, N. J.: Logos International, 1977.

Herman, Bridgid E. *Creative Prayer.* Wheaton, Ill.: Tyndale House Publishers, 1974.

Herring, Ralph. *The Cycle of Prayer.* Wheaton, Ill,: Tyndale House Publishers, 1974.

Hession, Roy. *The Calvary Road.* Fort Washington, Penn.: Christian Literature Crusade, n.d.

Howard, Walden. *Nine Roads to Renewal.* Waco, Tex.: Word Books, 1967.

Hubbard, David A. *The Problem With Prayer Is.* Wheaton, Ill.: Tyndale House Publishers, 1972.

Huegel, F. J. *The Ministry of Intercession.* Minneapolis: Bethany House Publishers, 1967.

————. *Prayer's Deeper Secrets.* Grand Rapids: Zondervan, 1959.

————. *Successful Praying.* Minneapolis: Bethany House Publishers, 1967.

Humbard, Rex. *Praying With Power.* Grand Rapids: New Hope Press, 1975.

Jones, E. Stanley. *Victorious Living.* Nashville: Abingdon Press, 1936.

Kenyon, E. W. *In His Presence.* Lynnwood, Wash.: Gospel Publishing Society, 1969.

Kimmel, Jo. *Steps to Prayer Power.* Nashville: Abingdon Press, 1972.

The Kneeling Christian. Grand Rapids: Zondervan, 1945.

Laubach, Frank C. *Prayer, The Mightiest Force in the World.* Old Tappan, N. J.: Revell, 1959.

Lavender, John Allan. *Why Prayers Are Unanswered.* Valley Forge, Penn.: Judson Press, 1967.

Lawrence, Brother. *Practice of the Presence of God.* Old Tappan, N. J.: Revell, 1956.

Lawson, Gilchrist. *Deeper Experiences of Famous Christians.* Anderson, Ind.: Warner Press, 1911.

Lindsell, Harold. *When You Pray.* Grand Rapids: Baker Book House, 1975.

McClure, J. G. *Intercessory Prayer.* Chicago: Moody Press, n.d.

McDonald, Hope. *Discovering How to Pray.* Grand Rapids: Zondervan, 1976.

McGraw, Francis A. *Praying Hyde.* Chicago: Moody Press, n.d.

Moody, D. L. *Prevailing Prayer.* Chicago: Moody Press, n.d.

Morgan, G. Campbell. *The Practice of Prayer*. Grand Rapids: Baker Book House, 1971.

Mueller, George. *Answers to Prayer*. Chicago: Moody Press, n.d.

Munger, R. *My Heart, Christ's Home*. Downers Grove, Ill.: InterVarsity Press, n.d.

Murray, Andrew. *The Ministry of Intercession*. Westwood, N. J.: Fleming H. Revell, Co., 1952.

———. *The Prayer Life*. Chicago: Moody Press, n.d.

———. *With Christ in the School of Prayer*. Old Tappan, N. J.: Revell, 1953.

Nee, Watchman. *The Normal Christian Life*. Fort Washington, Penn.: Christian Literature Crusade, 1961–63.

Neighbor, Ralph Webster. *The Touch of the Spirit*. Nashville: Broadman Press, 1972.

Newall, William Whiting. *Revivals, How and When*. New York: A. C. Armstrong and Sons, 1882.

Orr, James Edwin. *Campus Aflame*. Glendale, Calif.: Regal Books, 1972.

Parker, William R., and Elaine St. Johns. *Prayer Can Change Your Life*. Old Tappan, N. J.: Revell, 1975.

Payne, Thomas. *Prayer—The Greatest Force on Earth*. Chicago: Moody Press, n.d.

Pittenger, Norman. *Praying Today*. Grand Rapids: Eerdman's, 1974.

Prater, Arnold. *You Can Pray as You Ought*. Nashville: Nelson, 1977.

Ravenhill, Leonard. *Revival God's Way*. Minneapolis: Bethany House Publishers, 1983.

———. *Revival Praying*. Minneapolis: Bethany House Publishers, 1974.

———. *Why Revival Tarries*. Minneapolis: Bethany House Publishers.

Redpath, Alan. *Victorious Praying*. Old Tappan, N. J.: Revell, 1957.

Reidhead, Paris. *Beyond Petition*. Minneapolis: Bethany House Publishers, 1974.

Rinker, Rosalind. *Prayer: Conversing With God*. Grand Rapids: Zondervan, 1959.

Ryle, J. C. *A Call to Prayer*. Grand Rapids: Baker Book House, 1976.

Sanders, J. Oswald. *Prayer Power Unlimited*. Minneapolis: World Wide Publications, 1977.

Sheen, Fulton J. *Life of Christ*. Garden City, N. Y.: Image Books, 1977.

Shoemaker, Helen Smith. *The Secret of Effective Prayer*. Waco, Tex.: Word Books, 1967.

Shoemaker, Samuel Moor. *By the Power of God*. New York: Harper & Row, 1954.

———. *Revive Thy Church*. New York: Harper, 1948.

———. *With the Holy Spirit and With Fire*. New York: Harper, 1960.

Sims, A. *George Mueller: Man of Faith*. Chicago: Moody Press, n.d.

Spurgeon, Charles H. *Effective Prayer*. London: Evangelical Press, n.d.

————. *Lectures to My Students*. Grand Rapids: Baker Book House, 1977.

————. *Twelve Sermons on Prayer*. Grand Rapids: Baker Book House, 1971.

Stedman, Ray C. *Jesus Teaches on Prayer*. Waco, Tex.: Word Books, 1976.

Steere, Douglas V. *Dimensions of Prayer*. New York: Harper & Row, 1963.

Strauss, Lehman. *Sense and Nonsense About Prayers*. Chicago: Moody Press, 1976.

Taylor, Jack. *The Key to Triumphant Living*. Nashville: Broadman Press, 1971.

Taylor, Jack R. *Prayer: Life's Limitless Reach*. Nashville: Broadman Press, 1977.

Thielicke, Helmut. *Our Heavenly Father*. Grand Rapids: Baker Book House, 1974.

Torrey, R. A. *How to Pray*. New York: Fleming H. Revell and Co., 1900.

————. *The Power of Prayer*. Grand Rapids: Zondervan, 1974.

Townsend, Anne J. *Prayer Without Pretending*. Chicago: Moody Press, 1976.

Tozer, A. W. *The Knowledge of the Holy*. New York: Harper & Row, 1975.

Wallis, Arthur. *God's Chosen Fast*. Fort Washington, Penn.: Christian Literature Crusade, n.d.

————. *Jesus Prayed*. Fort Washington, Penn.: Christian Literature Crusade, 1966.

Whyte, Alexander. *Lord, Teach Us to Pray*. Grand Rapids: Baker Book House, 1976.